PRESBYTERIAN LAW
FOR THE LOCAL CHURCH

[*Fifth Edition*]

PRESBYTERIAN LAW

FOR THE

LOCAL CHURCH

A *Handbook for Church Officers and Members*

EDITED BY EUGENE CARSON BLAKE

A treatment of Presbyterian law limited to the topics and questions which regularly confront the officers and members of the particular church based upon the Constitution of The United Presbyterian Church in the United States of America and the Acts and Deliverances of the General Assembly.

Revised 1959

Published for the Office of the General Assembly by the General Division of Publication of the Board of Christian Education of The United Presbyterian Church in the United States of America

Library of Congress Catalog Card No. 59–8521

PRINTED IN THE UNITED STATES OF AMERICA

CONTENTS

PREFACE

The 164th General Assembly of the Presbyterian Church in the United States of America, meeting in New York City in May, 1952, directed the Stated Clerk to proceed to the editing and publishing of a new *Manual of Presbyterian Law for Church Officers and Members.* The present manual is, therefore, not a revision of the manual first published in 1927, but a new book based directly on the Constitution and on the Acts and Deliverances of the General Assembly.

The scope of this handbook is sharply limited, as directed by the General Assembly, to those parts of Presbyterian law which apply regularly to the problems confronting a particular church. The arrangement of the material is entirely new, being set forth in chapters so designed and in such order that those unfamiliar with the general law of the Church may most easily find authoritative answers to their questions to the end that the particular churches shall conduct their life and business in a Presbyterian way.

It is the hope of the editor that this new arrangement, together with the topical index, will enable all church officers and members to learn easily and quickly their rights and duties in the church. It should be remembered, however, that the basic law of the Presbyterian Church is contained in the Constitution and in the Digest.

Whenever, therefore, a problem of a particular church
reaches beyond the particular church to the rights and
responsibilities of the presbytery, synod, or General Assembly, it is assumed that the Constitution and the Digest
will be consulted as authoritative. One of the perennial
difficulties in the use of the earlier manual was that it was
sometimes consulted when the Constitution and the Digest should have been used. And, since it attempted to
cover a much broader field than the present handbook,
it was difficult for those who did not know the law already to find in it the answers to their questions.

Three kinds of type are used in the body of this book.
All quotations from the Constitution itself, which is the
basic law of the Church, are in italics. The Acts and Deliverances of the General Assembly, which are subordinate
to the Constitution which is subject only to the Scriptures themselves, are quoted in boldface type and have
the force of law until and unless a subsequent General
Assembly reverses or modifies them by a new judicial decision or by a new deliverance. The rest of the body of the
book is printed in ordinary type and is the opinion and
interpretation of the editor, who, as Stated Clerk, is, when
called upon, **to give opinions and interpretations of the
Constitutional provisions of the Church and of the Acts
and Deliverances of the General Assembly.**

Upon the adoption of the new Constitution in 1958,
on the occasion of the merger of the Presbyterian Church
in the United States of America with the United Presbyterian Church of North America, a Companion and Sup-
plement to the Fourth Edition of *Presbyterian Law for
the Local Church* was prepared, bringing all changes and
references into harmony with the new Constitution.
These changes have been made a part of this Fifth Edition. It should be noted that "United" is not always
added in such terms as "Presbyterian law," "Presbyterian
order," nor even in "Presbyterian Church" or "Presby-

terian church," since such usage has been common in both Churches.

The editor would here express his appreciation of the invaluable assistance given him in this task by Dr. Edward B. Shaw and Dr. Samuel W. Shane, the assistant editors, and by Mr. John Ribble and the other representatives of the Division of Publication of the Board of Christian Education who have co-operated so ably and harmoniously to produce this volume.

EUGENE CARSON BLAKE,
Stated Clerk of the General Assembly.

LIST OF ABBREVIATIONS

C.—Confession of Faith

G.—Form of Government

D.—Book of Discipline

W.—Directory for Worship

M.—Minutes of The General Assembly of The United Presbyterian Church in the United States of America

M. (U)—Minutes of The General Assembly of The United Presbyterian Church of North America

M. (P)—Minutes of The General Assembly of The Presbyterian Church in the United States of America

Dig.—Digest of The United Presbyterian Church in the United States of America (1958)

Hist. Dig. (U)—Digest of The United Presbyterian Church in the United States of America, Vol. II (United Presbyterian Church of North America, Historical Section)

Hist. Dig. (P)—Digest of The United Presbyterian Church in the United States of America, Vol. II (Presbyterian Church in the United States of America, Historical Section)

C.W.—Book of Common Worship

G. & W. (U)—Indicates reference to Book of Government and Worship of The United Presbyterian Church of North America.

(P)—Indicates reference to Constitution of Presbyterian Church in the United States of America.

FORM OF REFERENCES

In order that the references in this manual may be in harmony with the new edition of the Constitution and Digest, it should be noted that references to the Constitution are uniformly noted, first with the initial as indicated in abbreviations on page 10, next a Roman numeral indicating the chapter, next an Arabic numeral indicating a numbered section, and finally, usually a small letter indicating paragraphs within a section. Thus a citation from the Form of Government, Chapter XX, Section 1, the third paragraph of the section, will read: G. XX, 1, c.

When Minutes of the General Assembly of the Presbyterian Church U.S.A. are cited, it is understood that the reference is to the Journal, since 1922 designated Part (Volume) I. For example, when a reference is made to page 85 of Part I of the Minutes of 1927, the form of the citation will be: M. 1927, p. 85, retaining the reference form used in earlier years. If reference is made to Part II, Board Reports, or to Part III, Statistics (separated from the Journal in 1952), the citation will specify exactly. When Minutes of the General Assembly of the United Presbyterian Church N. A. are cited, it is understood that the reference is to the page in the single volume in which the Minutes were published until 1956, from which time the references apply to Part II of the Minutes.

I

BASIC PRINCIPLES

The United Presbyterian Church in the United States of America is a single and united body which claims to be a part of the visible Church catholic. (See C. XXV, 2.)

It does not claim to be the whole Church and seeks cooperation and fellowship with all Churches that are loyal to Jesus Christ as divine Lord and Savior.

It attempts to base all its beliefs and practices on the Scriptures of the Old and New Testaments, the books of which *are given bv inspiration of God, to be the rule of faith and life.* [C. I, 2.]

It is clearly a Church of law, which is not, however, to be understood as being opposed to love or spirit, but rather as opposed to disorder and injustice which so easily pervert right human relationships when authority is personal, in individuals or in groups, or when there is no accepted way of deciding issues that inevitably arise among men, however much they may be committed to Jesus Christ and to one another.

The law of The United Presbyterian Church in the United States of America presupposes a fellowship of men and women with their children in voluntary covenanted relationship with one another and with God through Jesus Christ. The law rests upon the fellowship and is not designed to work without trust and love. Many a particular Presbyterian church carries on effective work and witness for Jesus Christ for years without its members or even its officers being especially conscious of the law of the Church. When, however, occasions do arise when the members of a particular church find that they differ deeply on some issue of belief, policy, or action, it is important that they realize that they belong to a Church of law which sets forth the right way in which such differences ought to be resolved. Sometimes, inevitably, the decision will go at last against the position and even the sense of justice of some in the church. It is here that Constitutional law protects both the minority in proper freedom and the majority in the exercise of necessary decision. And, unless the actions taken are such that they violate the conscience of the member as enlightened by the Scriptures under the guidance of the Holy Spirit, it is the duty of that member to abide by the decision of the majority in the highest court of the Church to which the decision is legally appealed. If the actions so taken are contrary to prayerful conscience, there is as a last resort the possibility of renouncing the fellowship, which is voluntary.

Very early in the history of our Church, even before the General Assembly was established, the plan of reunion of the Synod of New York and Philadelphia contained the following sentences: **That when any matter is determined by major vote, every member shall either actively concur with or passively submit to such determination or if his conscience permit him to do neither, he shall, after sufficient liberty modestly to reason and remonstrate, peaceably withdraw from our communion without attempting to make any schism. Provided always that this shall be understood to extend only to such determination as the body shall judge indispensable in doctrine or Presbyterian government.** [Hist. Dig. (P), p. 1310.] In the union of the Associate and Associate Reformed Churches to form The United Presbyterian Church of North America, one basis of union was:

Whereas, It is agreed between the two Churches that the forbearance in love which is required by the law of God will be exercised towards any brethren who may not be able fully to subscribe the standards of the United Church, while they do not determinedly oppose them, but follow the things which make for peace, and things whereby one may edify another; *Resolved:*—That these Churches . . . [Hist. Dig. (U), Ch. CVII.]

Freedom and responsibility under law are the two-part heritage of all the members of the Presbyterian Church. Our fathers gave us a Church which, despite its failures and sins, has been blessed by Jesus Christ, its only head. (See C. XXV, 6.) The Preliminary Principles of the Presbyterian Form of Government are so important to the understanding of what follows in this book that they are quoted in full as found in the Form of Government, Chapter I. This chapter as it appears below, with the exception of the first sentence, was first drawn up by the Synod of New York and Philadelphia (then the highest body of our Church) and prefixed to the Form of Government, etc., as published by that body in 1788. In that year, after arranging the plan on which the Presbyterian Church is now governed, the Synod was divided into four Synods, and gave place to the General Assembly, which met for the first time in 1789.

The United Presbyterian Church in the United States of America, in presenting to the Christian public the system of union and the form of government and discipline which they have adopted, have thought proper to state, by way of introduction, a few of the general principles by which they have been governed in the formation of the plan. This, it is hoped, will in some measure prevent those rash misconstructions, and uncandid reflections, which usually proceed from an imperfect view of any subject; as well as make the several parts of the system plain, and the whole perspicuous and fully understood.

They are unanimously of opinion:

1. That "God alone is Lord of the conscience, and hath left it free from the doctrines and commandments of men which are in any thing contrary to his Word, or beside it, in matters of faith or worship." Therefore they consider the rights of private judgment, in all matters that respect religion, as universal and unalienable: they do not even wish to see any religious constitution aided by the civil power, further than may be necessary for protection and security, and, at the same time, be equal and common to all others.

2. That, in perfect consistency with the above principle of common right, every Christian Church, or union or association of particular churches, is entitled to declare the terms of admission into its communion, and the qualifications of its ministers and members, as well as the whole system of its internal goverment which Christ hath appointed; that in the exercise of this right they may, notwithstanding, err, in making the terms of communion either too lax or too narrow yet, even in this case, they do not infringe upon the liberty or the rights of others, but only make an improper use of their own.

3. That our blessed Savior, for the edification of the visible Church, which is his body, hath appointed officers, not only to preach the gospel and administer the sacraments, but also to exercise discipline, for the preservation both of truth and duty; and that it is incumbent upon these officers, and upon the whole Church, in whose name they act, to censure or cast out the erroneous and scandalous, observing, in all cases, the rules contained in the Word of God.

4. That truth is in order to goodness; and the great touchstone of truth, its tendency to promote holiness, according to our Savior's rule, "By their fruits ye shall know them." And that no opinion can be either more pernicious or more absurd than that which brings truth and

falsehood upon a level, and represents it as of no consequence what a man's opinions are. On the contrary, they are persuaded that there is an inseparable connection between faith and practice, truth and duty. Otherwise it would be of no consequence either to discover truth or to embrace it.

5. That while under the conviction of the above principle they think it necessary to make effectual provision that all who are admitted as teachers be sound in the faith, they also believe that there are truths and forms with respect to which men of good characters and principles may differ. And in all these they think it the duty both of private Christians and societies to exercise mutual forbearance towards each other.

6. That though the character, qualifications, and authority of church officers are laid down in the Holy Scriptures, as well as the proper method of their investiture and institution, yet the election of the persons to the exercise of this authority, in any particular society, is in that society.

7. That all church power, whether exercised by the body in general or in the way of representation by delegated authority, is only ministerial and declarative; that is to say, that the Holy Scriptures are the only rule of faith and manners; that no church judicatory ought to pretend to make laws to bind the conscience in virtue of their own authority; and that all their decisions should be founded upon the revealed will of God. Now though it will easily be admitted that all synods and councils may err, through the frailty inseparable from humanity, yet there is much greater danger from the usurped claim of making laws than from the right of judging upon laws already made, and common to all who profess the gospel, although this right, as necessity requires in the present state, be lodged with fallible men.

8. Lastly, that, if the preceding Scriptural and rational

principles be steadfastly adhered to, the vigor and strictness of its discipline will contribute to the glory and happiness of any Church. Since ecclesiastical discipline must be purely moral or spiritual in its object, and not attended with any civil effects, it can derive no force whatever but from its own justice, the approbation of an impartial public, and the countenance and blessing of the great Head of the Church Universal.

II

THE DUTIES AND RIGHTS OF THE CONGREGATION

A *particular church consists of a number of professing Christians, with their children, voluntarily associated together for divine worship and godly living, agreeably to the Holy Scriptures, and submitting to a certain form of government.*

A *particular church can be organized only by the authority of the presbytery.* [G. IV, 1-2.]

A. DUTIES

1. These members by their own voluntary association together have certain duties that they owe by the very fact of their membership. They, *by profession, are bound to maintain an holy fellowship and communion, in the worship of God, and in performing such other spiritual services as tend to their mutual edification; as also in relieving each other in outward things, according to their several abilities and necessities. Which communion, as God offereth opportunity, is to be extended unto all those who, in every place, call upon the name of the Lord Jesus.* [C. XXVI, 2.]

2. In addition to the above general obligations of membership, the members of a particular church voluntarily put themselves under the leadership of their officers when they elect them. The session (which consists of the pas-

tor, or pastors, and active ruling elders) is the governing body in a particular church. (See Chapter IV of this manual.) The duties of the members of a particular church will, therefore, vary with the considered requests and decisions made by their own session. When elders are ordained or installed in a particular church, the ordaining or installing minister asks the members of the congregation present, *Do you, the members of this church, acknowledge and receive this brother (sister) as a ruling elder . . . and do you promise to yield him (her) all that honor, encouragement, and obedience in the Lord to which his (her) office, according to the Word of God and the Constitution of this Church, entitles him (her)?* [G. XVII, 7.]

3. The members of a particular church also have obligations to their pastor (or associate pastor) consonant with the affirmative replies given to the installing officer of the presbytery at installation. These questions are:

(1) *Do you, the people of this church, continue to profess your readiness to receive A.B., whom you have called to be your pastor (or associate pastor)?*

(2) *Do you promise to receive the word of truth from his mouth with meekness and love and to submit to him in the due exercise of discipline?*

(3) *Do you promise to encourage him in his labors, and to assist his endeavors for your instruction and spiritual edification?*

(4) *And do you engage to continue to him while he is your pastor (or associate pastor) that competent worldly maintenance which you have promised, and to furnish him with whatever you may see needful for the honor of religion and for his comfort among you?* [G. XX, 13.]

4. The members of a particular church also have a special annual obligation in relation to the compensation to the

pastor (or associate pastor): *We promise and oblige our-selves to review with you the adequacy of this compensation annually, prior to the adoption of the church budget.* [G. XX, 6.] This annual review should be definitely related to the preparation of the annual budget. (See Chapter VI, A, 2, f, in this manual.)

5. The members of a particular church have also the duty to attend regularly called congregational meetings to deliberate and vote upon questions properly brought before them.

B. RIGHTS

1. The rights of the congregation of a particular Presbyterian church are limited by the above duties and by the fact that the governing principle in the Presbyterian Church is representative and constitutional democracy and not pure democracy or unlimited majority rule.

2. The members of the congregation of a particular Presbyterian church properly exercise their rights by vote in congregational meetings, both ecclesiastical and corporation, or, in some states, in a meeting which is both, the ecclesiastical meeting being recognized by the state law as a legal corporation meeting.

3. The rules governing an ecclesiastical meeting (and meetings which are both ecclesiastical and corporation) are as follows:

a. A congregational meeting may be called in the following ways:

(1) By the session according to bylaws previously adopted by the congregation for the annual meeting. If there is a discretionary choice of place, date, or hour in the bylaws, the session should by formal action set the particular hour and date and place.

(2) By action of the session for a special meeting.

(3) By order of the presbytery for a special meeting.

b. *Public notice of the time, place, and purpose of the meeting shall be given at least one week prior to the appointed time.* [G. XX, 1, a.]

Although the above reference to required Constitutional notice is limited to a meeting called for the purpose of electing a pastor, nevertheless, it is proper that all annual or special meetings of the congregation should have the same notice. (See Dig., p. A922; G. & W. (U), 204.)

c. Except in the annual meeting, at which any Constitutional action may be taken, the business of a congregational meeting must be confined to those items specifically listed in the call for the meeting. (See Dig., p. A245; G. & W. (U), 205.)

d. The pastor, who is, by virtue of his office, moderator of the session, shall preside at all congregational meetings (ecclesiastical) with the following exceptions (see G. & W. (U), 207 (2); Dig., p. A924):

(1) In his absence or illness the session may ask another minister, a member of the same presbytery, to preside.

(2) When a church is without a pastor, the moderator of the session appointed by the presbytery shall preside at all congregational meetings, unless it is inconvenient for him to be present without neglect of other duties, in which case the session with his consent may invite another member of the same presbytery to preside. The Constitution requires that *when a congregation is convened for the election of a pastor . . . the moderator of the session or some other minister of the same presbytery appointed by him shall preside, and the clerk of the session shall act as secretary.* [G. XX, 2, a.] Such arrangements should be made through the ministerial relations committee of the presbytery.

(3) When the subject to be discussed is the possible dissolution of the pastoral relationship, or difficulties between pastor and session or congregation, the pastor should invite, with the approval of the session, another minister of the same presbytery to preside. This arrangement should also be made in consultation with the ministerial relations committee of the presbytery.

(4) When the congregation is reviewing the pastor's compensation (see Form of Government, Chapter XX, Sec. 6), the pastor may be excused and the clerk of the session may preside for this purpose only. It is to be noted that the clerk of the session may, under these circumstances, allow no discussion but that which is specifically related to a motion to raise, decrease, or continue the compensation of the pastor. If there is any disposition on the part of the congregation to wish to discuss dissolution of the pastoral relationship or difficulties between pastor and session or congregation, the clerk of session is directed to inform the congregation that such discussion is out of order and that he, as clerk, will present to the session a recommendation that a congregational meeting be called to discuss any general matters as to the relationship of the pastor to the congregation, but that it must be presided over according to provision (3) above. [M. (P) 1957, p. 282.]

e. The clerk of the session shall be secretary of the meetings of the congregation. In case of his inability to attend, the session shall designate a secretary in his stead.

f. All communicant members of a particular church, of whatever age, in good and regular standing, but no others, shall be eligible to vote at congregational meetings held for ecclesiastical purposes. (See G. XVII, 4; XX, 2; XXXII, 6; G. & W. (U), 139; Dig., pp. A741 f.)

g. Meetings of the congregation should be conducted in accordance with the General Rules for Judicatories adopted by the General Assembly of The United Presbyterian Church in the United States of America, so far as they apply, and, when they do not apply, according to the usual legislative rules of order. (See Appendix G of this manual for the General Rules for Judicatories. See Appendix A for suggested bylaws of a congregation for a meeting.)

h. Voting by proxy is not allowed. (See G. V, 4.)

j. Rules 1 and 82 of the General Rules for Judicatories require all meetings to be opened and closed with prayer.

4. The members of a particular church corporation and all its activities are subject to the various laws of the several states and to the charter or articles of incorporation of the particular church corporation. These latter must, however, be in harmony with and subject to the Constitution of The United Presbyterian Church in the United States of America.

5. The rules governing a corporation meeting are as follows:

a. A corporation meeting may be called in the following ways:

(1) By the board of trustees according to the bylaws of the corporation. When discretion is given as to the hour, date, or place of the annual meeting, the board of trustees should by formal action set the particular hour, date, and place. (See b below for required notice.)

(2) The board of trustees may call a special meeting of the corporation.

(3) The session may direct the board of trustees to call a special meeting of the corporation.

(4) The presbytery may direct the board of trustees to call a special meeting of the corporation.

b. *Unless otherwise provided for, all particular church corporation meetings shall be called by giving public notice thereof from the pulpit on the two successive Sun-*

days next preceding the day of such meeting. [G. XXXII, 10.]

c. At a special meeting of the corporation only such subjects may be considered as are specified in the call of the meeting. (See G. & W. (U), 205; M. (P), 1916, p. 244.)

d. The presiding officer and secretary at a corporation meeting shall be determined according to the bylaws of the corporation.

e. *The communicant members of a particular church in good and regular standing shall be entitled at all meetings of the church to vote on all matters affecting the ecclesiastical affairs of the church, and also on all matters affecting the corporate affairs unless otherwise provided by the laws of the state governing its incorporation.* [G. XXXII, 6.]

f. *Voting by proxy shall not be permitted, except in those states where voting by proxy in religious corporations is expressly required by statute.* [G. XXXII, 11.]

g. For method of nomination and election of trustees, see this manual, Chapter III.

6. Under the Constitution of The United Presbyterian Church in the United States of America the powers of the congregation of a particular church are strictly limited to the following:

a. To elect a nominating committee to nominate a minister to the congregation for election as a pastor. (See Chapter IX of this manual.)

b. To elect a pastor or pastors. (See Chapter IX of this manual.)

c. To approve the terms of call to a pastor.

d. To authorize certain members to sign the call and to select members to prosecute it before presbytery. (See G. XX, 5, 7.)

e. To change the terms of the call of a pastor, subject

to approval by the presbytery.

f. To elect ruling elders and deacons. (See Chapter III of this manual.)

g. To indicate to presbytery its desire for a change in its pastor. (See G. XXI, 1.)

h. Through its corporation to elect trustees. (See Chapter III of this manual.)

j. To determine the number of members of the nominating committee to be elected annually, and the method of electing the majority of them. (See G. XVII, 1 (2); and Chapter III in this manual. See also item s, at the end of this chapter.)

k. To refuse to consent to the installation of a pastor. (See G. XX, 13, 14.)

l. To show cause by commissioners why the presbytery should not accept the resignation of a pastor. (See G. XXI, 1.)

m. *When any minister shall resign his charge by reason of age or incapacity for further labor, and the congregation shall be moved by affectionate regard for his person and gratitude for his ministry among them, to desire that he should continue to be associated with them in an honorary relation, they may, at a regularly called meeting, elect him as pastor emeritus, with or without honorarium, but with no pastoral authority or duty. This action shall be subject to the approval of presbytery, and shall take effect upon the formal dissolution of the pastoral relation.* [G. XXI, 2.]

n. To indicate a desire to unite with another church, or to refuse so to do. (See G. XII, 7.)

o. To indicate a desire to be divided into two congregations, or to refuse so to do. (See G. XII, 7.)

p. To memorialize presbytery concerning any matter needing action by that body.

q. To establish or alter its own rules (subject to the Constitution of The United Presbyterian Church in the

United States of America) as to such subjects as a quorum necessary to conduct business, etc. (See Appendixes A and B.)

r. To consider and vote upon any question which the session or the trustees, or both, bring properly before it.

s. To request presbytery to exempt the congregation from one or more of the requirements of Form of Government, Chapter XVII, Section 1 (1) and (2), but only if the congregation is limited in membership. (See G. XVII, 1 (5) and Chapter III, A, 2 (5), of this manual.)

t. To vote to lodge all the administrative responsibility, both spiritual and corporate, in one body, which shall be the session. (See G. XI, 7, b.)

u. To choose a majority of the members of the representative nominating committee of the congregation. (See G. XVII, 1 (2); and Chapter III, following.)

III

THE ELECTION OF CHURCH OFFICERS

A. RULING ELDERS

1. *As there were in Old Testament times elders of the people for the purpose of government, so in the New Testament Church, Christ has provided others beside the ministers of the Word with gifts and commission to govern, which officers are entitled ruling elders.*

Those who fill this office ought to be blameless in life and sound in the faith; they should be persons of wisdom and discretion; and in their walk and conversation should be examples to the flock.

Ruling elders, the immediate representatives of the people, are chosen by them, that, in association with the pastors or ministers, they may exercise government and discipline, and take the oversight of the spiritual interests of the particular church, and also of the Church generally, when called thereunto. [G. IX, 1, 3, 4, a.]

2. *Every congregation shall elect persons (either men or women) from among its members in full communion to the office of ruling elder, and to the office of deacon, or either of them, in the mode most approved and in use in that congregation, subject, however, to the following provisions:*

(1) *No ruling elder shall be elected to the session for a term of more than three years, nor shall a ruling elder*

serve on the session for consecutive terms, either full or partial, aggregating more than six years. A ruling elder having been elected to the session for consecutive terms aggregating six years shall be ineligible to serve thereon for a further term until at least one year has elapsed from the expiration of the last term for which he was elected. A particular church may provide for a period of ineligibility after one full term. There shall always be three classes of ruling elders on the session as nearly equal in number as possible, one class only of which shall expire each year and terms shall always be for three years, except when it is necessary to elect some for shorter terms in order to equalize the numbers in the classes or to fill vacancies.

(2) Nominations shall be made by a representative nominating committee of communicant members of the church. Not more than two members of this committee shall be designated by and from the session, one of whom shall be named by the session as chairman. One member of this committee shall be designated by and from the board of deacons, if there be such a board, and one by and from the board of trustees, if there be such a board. Other members of the committee, in sufficient number to constitute a majority thereof (exclusive of the pastor), shall be chosen by the congregation, or by such organizations within the church as the congregation may designate. In addition, the pastor shall be a member of this committee ex officio but without vote. The nominating committee shall be chosen annually.

(3) Full opportunity shall always be accorded at the congregational meeting for nominations by any eligible voter.

(4) The foregoing provisions shall apply to the nomination, election, and tenure of deacons.

(5) *A particular church may be exempted from one or more of the requirements of provisions* (1) *and* (2) *above at the discretion of the presbytery, by a three-fourths vote, but only on the ground that its membership is so limited as to make such requirements unfeasible. Such exemption shall be granted for not more than three years at a time, but shall be subject to renewal on the same ground by a three-fourths vote and to revocation at any time by a majority vote. Provision* (2) *shall not apply to a new church in the process of being organized.* [G. XVII, 1.]

The foregoing, Section 1 of Chapter XVII of the Form of Government, is quoted here in full because of its importance. Exemption from any of the requirements of provisions (1) and (2) may be granted to a particular church by presbytery only in accordance with the procedure outlined in (5) above. It is incumbent upon churches to make every effort to put into effect any and all feasible requirements.

3. The principles of the rotary system of membership of session may be thus summarized:

a. The office of ruling elder is perpetual.

b. The full term to which anyone may be elected is three years.

c. The period of continuous active service is limited to six years, precluding election to a full term if even a brief partial term preceded a full one.

d. This period may be further limited by any particular church to one full term (plus any previous partial term).

e. After one inactive year an ordained ruling elder is eligible for re-election. (For preparation of eligibility lists, see 9, below.)

f. The foregoing principles apply also to deacons.

g. The foregoing principles, except "a," apply also to trustees. (See G. XXXII, 8; and section C, below, in this chapter.)

h. Exemption from one or more of these requirements and/or those of subsection (2) in the Constitutional provision may be granted by presbytery to any particular church showing good reasons for such exemption. (See 11, below.)

4. The principles underlying the provisions for a nominating committee in the local church may be thus summarized:

a. Designation by the official boards of an experienced group of officers of the church, including the chairman.

b. Protection of the rights of the congregation by its election of a majority of the members of the committee outside the official boards.

c. Wider representation in consideration of possible officer material.

d. A unified approach to the task of making nominations.

e. Time and opportunity to consider and interview prospective nominees.

f. The counsel and advice of the pastor, *ex officio but without vote*.

g. Specified right of nomination from the floor by any eligible voter.

h. Exemption from one or more of these requirements and/or those of subsection 1 (1) in the Constitutional provision may be granted by presbytery to any particular church showing good reason for such exemption. (See 11, below.)

5. It is the province of the congregation to determine the number of the members of the nominating committee chosen by it, in addition to those designated by the official boards. The one requirement is that the number be greater than that of the designated group. The session may suggest the number, but the final decision rests with

the congregation. It should have some relation to the size of the congregation and the number of major organizations or groups of organizations in it.

6. The method of choosing the elected members of the nominating committee is also to be determined by the congregation, usually upon suggestion of the session; but directly or indirectly the congregation should choose. Various methods are employed, such as:

a. Each major organization or group of organizations is designated by the congregation to name a member of the committee.

b. The nominating committee elected the previous year nominates members at large for the nominating committee to succeed it.

c. A combination of plans "a" and "b" is used.

d. The nominations are made from the floor and the proper number elected by ballot.

e. In any case, it is always in order for any eligible voter to make nominations of eligible persons from the floor when the congregation is electing.

f. Those designated by the official boards in accordance with the Constitution are not subject to election, nor are those appointed by organizations designated by the congregation under plan "a." This includes the chairman and at most (three) other designated officers, together with the pastor, who *shall be a member of this committee ex officio but without vote.*

7. The time of choosing the elected members of the nominating committee is also determined by the congregation, usually upon the recommendation of the session. Suggested times are:

a. At each annual meeting of the congregation, to serve until the close of the following annual meeting.

b. At a regularly called meeting of the congregation at

least a month previous to the annual meeting.

c. In the case of delegation of power to organizations of the congregation, a definite time previous to the annual meeting may be fixed for such designation of members of the committee.

d. If the time is that of the same annual meeting at which the committee is to report, the election of the nominating committee should come early on the docket, and the committee should be excused to prepare its report. (This should never be done in a church of good size, as there is insufficient time to give proper consideration to this important task.)

8. The choice of the members of the nominating committee to be designated by the official boards and organizations should be made well in advance of the annual meeting so that at least these members of the committee, as individuals, may have opportunity to consider the necessary changes required or desirable in the official boards.

9. Eligibility lists of ruling elders and deacons should be kept. The appropriate custodian of these lists is the clerk of session, whose record should be considered the official one. The clerk should familiarize himself with the Constitutional provisions of Section 1 (1), and the summarization in 3, above, so that the list will be accurate. The appropriate custodian of the eligibility list of trustees is the secretary of the board of trustees, whose record should likewise be considered the official one. These lists should be in the hands of the designated chairman of the nominating committee as soon as possible after he has been named.

a. Ineligibility ordinarily is calculated as coming after two full terms, but may result from a full term added to a partial term; as continuous service for more than a total of six years is not permitted. However, several partial (unexpired) terms which would make the period of continuous service a total of not more than six years is permissible. *A particular church may provide for a period of ineligibility after one full term* (plus a possible previous partial term). [G. XVII, 1 (1).]

b. Previous service under life tenure is not included in the calculation of ineligibility.

10. The status of a ruling elder, so far as his (her) ordination is concerned, is not affected by any period of inactivity, whether for the year of ineligibility following six years of continuous service, or for a longer and indefinite period. Certain rights and privileges remain, as is indicated by the Constitution:

The limitations placed by Section 1 of this Chapter XVII upon the period for which ruling elders and deacons may be elected and may serve, apply to service on the session and the board of deacons, and such service is for convenience of expression sometimes referred to in this Form of Government as "active service." In all other respects the offices of ruling elder and deacon are perpetual and no one can lay either office aside at pleasure or be divested thereof except by deposition. Without limiting the generality of the foregoing, a ruling elder, once ordained, is not divested of office by the circumstance that he (she) is not re-elected to serve upon the session of a particular church, or by the fact that he (she) ceases to be a member of that church, and he (she) shall be entitled to represent in presbytery the particular church of which he (she) is at any time a member when appointed by its session and to serve as a member of synod and of the General Assembly when duly elected as such. [G. XVII, 2.]

For suggestions on the service and activities of ruling elders and other officers during the required "inactive" years, see Chapter IV, A, 8.

STATEMENT AND REQUEST

of the _____ Church of _____
to the Presbytery of _____

1. The present membership of this church is _____.
2. There are _____ ruling elders in active service.
3. The _____ Church is _____.

(Give the status or nature of the church, such as: rural, National Missions, federated, larger parish, racial group, language group, interracial, center city, inner city, etc.)

4. The special circumstances are: _____

_____

(State the circumstances, nature of the area, etc., of the church which would affect its growth or stability, such as: rural area with population static or declining; National Missions project with emphasis upon Sunday church school, community service, etc.; changing area with encroaching commercial and/or industrial invasion, with large percentage of members living at a distance and local membership dwindling; large turnover of membership due to the nature of the area; or other factors which would work hardship if all the provisions of Section 1 (1) and (2) were followed.)

In the light of the facts and circumstances stated above, and in accordance with Form of Government, Chapter XVII, Section 1 (5), the _____ Church of _____ respectfully requests the Presbytery of _____ to grant exemption of this church from the following requirements of Form of Government, Chapter XVII, Section 1 (1) and (2), relating to the election of church officers: _____.

(List requirements of (1) and/or (2) which would work a hardship upon the church in its service and worship.)

Date of congregational meeting _____. Actual count of vote _____.

_____, *Clerk of Session*

Recommended action: _____
_____, *Chairman of Committee of Presbytery*

11. The session of a particular church that has questions as to the feasibility of some of the requirements in provisions (1) and (2) of Section 1 should give careful consideration to the matter. If after such consideration it is the judgment of the session that the limitations of the congregation warrant such action, the approved form of the Statement and Request, on the preceding page, should be submitted to the annual meeting of the congregation for approval and later presentation to presbytery for action by that body.

12. A careful reading of the whole of Section 1 of the Form of Government, above, makes plain certain facts.

a. A new church in process of being organized is automatically exempted from provision (2).

b. The hope is that all churches may eventually achieve the full Constitutional provisions of (1) and (2).

c. The request for exemption must come by vote of the congregation.

d. Exemption is to be granted by presbytery only on the grounds indicated in (5): that the membership of the church *is so limited as to make such requirements unfeasible*.

e. Presbytery, by three-fourths vote, may grant exemption for not more than three years; renewable in like manner.

f. No penalties may be laid upon a church because of its Constitutional exemption by presbytery under provision (5) of this Section 1.

13. General matters relating to ruling elders and membership on the session.

a. A church may not have term eldership and life eldership at the same time. (See Dig., p. A751.)

b. **When a ruling elder in the Presbyterian Church, by removal or otherwise, terminates his connection with** the session by whom he was ordained, does he require installation before he can regularly exercise again the office in the same church or in any other one? Answered in the affirmative. [Dig., p. A761.] (See also Dig., p. A749.)

As an interpretation of the law of the Church regarding the status of an elder who has received a certificate of dismission and still retains it, it is declared that, though still an elder, he is not a member of any session, and can become such only in the ordinary way, namely, by election and installation. [Dig., A762.]

c. If one of the exemptions granted by the presbytery of jurisdiction to a particular church is in regard to the use of a nominating committee, then the session may nominate persons to the congregation for vacancies to be filled. (See Dig., p. A733; G. & W. (U), 174.) Otherwise, the nomination must now be made by a nominating committee. (See G. XVII, 1 (2).) In any case nominations from the floor are always in order. (See G. XVII, 1 (3).)

d. Who may be elected?

(1) Men or women, communicants in good standing of years of discretion, are eligible to the office of ruling elder. (See G. XVII, 1.)

(2) They must be willing to serve and to answer in the affirmative Questions 1–7 in the order for ordination. (See G. XVII, 6, 7, and also C.W., Form and Order for the Ordination of Elders.)

(3) Ultimately the congregation must be the judge of the personal life and the qualifications of character of those whom they would choose as their representatives in the government of the church. This must be basically within the discretion of the members of the congregation or else their right to be represented is contravened.

(4) An elder must be elected to the session of the church. He may not be elected an elder in general in order to make him eligible to serve in presbytery, synod, or General Assembly.

B. DEACONS

In addition to the ruling elders, deacons are ordinary and perpetual officers of the church. (See G. X, 1.) The rules for their nomination and election are the same as those which apply to ruling elders as listed in section A, 2–12, except that the board of deacons does not have the provisional right of nomination to the congregation noted in A, 13, c, above, which right in the case of deacons is also reserved to the session.

C. TRUSTEES

Trustees are, strictly speaking, not officers of the church but rather officers of the church corporation. (See G. XXXII and Chapter VI of this manual.) The rules for their election and nomination will vary, therefore, according to state law and the charter or articles of incorporation and the bylaws under the state law in the several states. The charters and bylaws are, however, subject to the Constitution of The United Presbyterian Church in the United States of America in the following respect as regards election:

The term "trustees," as it is used in this Form of Government in relation to a particular church, designates such officers as shall be elected by the church to fulfill the requirements of civil law in respect to the church corporation, whether or not they are called trustees by the civil law. Trustees of a particular church shall be chosen at such time and in such manner as may be required by civil law, with two further conditions: (1) They shall be communicant members of said church, and (2) the provisions of Chapter XVII relating to the nomination, election, and tenure of ruling elders and deacons shall apply with equal force to trustees, except as the civil law may otherwise require; provided, however, that any trustee in office on May 23, 1952, may be retained in office during his term

*then current or any extension thereof, at the discretion of
the congregation; and further provided, that condition
(1) shall not apply to the National Presbyterian Church
of Washington D.C., wherein the General Assembly,
when incorporating the National Presbyterian Church,
specifically provided otherwise.* [G. XXXII, 8.]

It is understood that the extension of the tenure of
office of noncommunicant trustees includes as many consecutive terms as the congregation may determine, including, as consecutive, terms that are interrupted for a period
of ineligibility, but no longer, under a rotary system.

D. GENERAL

1. For the ordination of new elders and deacons and the
installation of those who have been ordained before (in
any congregation of this Church) and for a form of
public recognition of newly elected trustees, see *The Book
of Common Worship* under these headings. Until an
elected elder or deacon is ordained or installed, he is not
a member of the session or board of deacons and may not
legally participate in formal meetings. (See Dig., p. A747,
A758 ff.)

A ruling elder of a Reformed Church holding the
Presbyterian Order in correspondence with the General
Assembly, being received by certificate of dismission as a
communicant member of a congregation, if elected to
the session, may be installed without reordination, provided that he shall answer in the affirmative the questions required by the Form of Government in the ordination of ruling elders. [M. 1958, p. 445.]

2. With the adoption of the required term service and
rotation of membership in session and board of deacons,
the older process of removing a ruling elder who had become unacceptable to a majority of the congregation (see
G. & W. (U), 185; and G. XIII, 6, 7 (P)) has been abro-

gated, since no term of service may now extend beyond three years without re-election. Provision for retirement, however, is made.

3. *For good cause a ruling elder may resign from the session, with its consent. For good cause a deacon may resign from the board of deacons, with the consent of the session. On ceasing to be a communicant member of a particular church, a ruling elder in active service ceases to be a member of its session, and a deacon in active service ceases to be a member of its board of deacons.* [G. XVII, 3.]

4. A trustee who wishes to resign his office does so to the board of trustees, the resignation taking effect when accepted by that body.

5. *A church, if it so desires, may lodge all of the administrative responsibility, both spiritual and corporate, in one body, which shall be the session.* [G. XI, 7, b.]

IV

THE DUTIES AND RIGHTS OF THE SESSION

The session of a particular church consists of the pastor (or co-pastors) and the ruling elders in active service. [G. XI, 1.]

The relationship of an associate pastor to a congregation shall be dissolved by the presbytery when it dissolves the relationship of the pastor in any particular church, or in case of the death of the pastor, except that upon request of the congregation the relationship may be continued until a new pastor is called, whereupon it shall be then dissolved, unless upon renewed request by the congregation it is further continued by the presbytery. An associate pastor shall be directed in his work by the pastor in consultation with the session. [G. XX, 1, d.]

An associate pastor is not a voting member of the session, but may sit in the session with full right of discussion on all matters. It is, however, proper for the session to ask an associate pastor to retire when it desires to discuss the work of the associate pastor himself, since an associate pastor takes his direction for his work from the pastor, in consultation with the elders. An associate pastor may moderate a meeting of the session on the invitation of the pastor, with the consent of the elders. (G. IV, 2 (P), having now the significance of a deliverance of the General Assembly (P).)

It is important to remember at the outset that a session basically consists of two parts: the ruling elders elected by the communicant members of a particular church as their representatives and the pastor or pastors installed in that church by the presbytery (but only at the request of the congregation). Apart from the ruling elders, the pastor has very little authority of his own in a Presbyterian church (see Chapter VII of this manual); apart from the pastor or a substitute minister provided by the presbytery, the ruling elders have practically no authority as a group or as individuals. A basic principle of Presbyterian government is that authority is lodged in ordered groups and not in individuals. A further general principle of Presbyterian government is that, under the Constitution, these responsible and ordered groups of men and women have authority sufficient to exercise their responsibility, but their official actions are subject to the Constitution of the Church and to appeal or complaint to higher bodies by minority members. Furthermore, their actions are subject to review and reversal (subject to the Constitution) by these higher bodies (judicatories), which are in our Church—the presbyteries, the synods, and the General Assembly.

The duties and rights outlined in this chapter are therefore to be understood as the duties and rights of the whole session made up of the two essential parts noted above. The mode of the election of ruling elders is treated in Chapter III and the calling of a pastor in Chapter IX.

Since it is the session, as an organized and ordered group, which has responsibility and authority (duties and rights) in a particular Presbyterian church, the body of this chapter is divided into two main parts: A. Rules for Session Meetings; B. The Authority and Responsibility of the Session.

A. RULES FOR SESSION MEETINGS

1. How called? A meeting of the session may be called in the following ways (see G. XI, 11):

a. By the pastor at his own discretion.

b. By any two or more elders through the pastor, who shall convene the session when so requested.

c. By the presbytery.

d. According to a Standing Rule adopted by the session.

2. Quorum. *Two ruling elders, if there be so many, with the pastor, if there be any, shall be necessary to constitute a quorum; unless the ruling elders number nine or more, when one third of the ruling elders, with the pastor, if there be any, shall be necessary to constitute a quorum.* [G. XI, 2.] If a church has no installed pastor, it is nevertheless *expedient at every meeting of the session that there be a presiding minister. . . . When it is impracticable to procure the attendance of such a moderator, the session of a church without a pastor may elect one of its own members to preside, except in judicial cases, when a minister of the same presbytery shall preside.* [G. XI, 4.] The above is quoted here to make it very clear that the quorum may be challenged if no presiding minister is present, and the actions of such a meeting, if later the subject of complaint or appeal, may thereby be voided. In any case, at such a meeting without a minister moderator, no action may be taken that would affect the status of any church member.

3. Who may preside?

a. *The pastor of the church shall be the moderator of the session. When for prudential reasons it may appear advisable that some other minister should be invited to preside, the pastor shall, with the concurrence of the session, invite another minister belonging to the same presbytery to preside. In the case of the sickness or absence of the pastor the same expedient may be adopted; or the session, the approval of the pastor first having been obtained, may convene and elect one of its own members to preside, except in judicial cases, when a minister of the same presbytery shall preside.* [G. XI, 3.] (See also page 41 in this manual, which deals with the status of an associate pastor.)

b. *When a church is without a pastor, the moderator of the session shall be either the minister appointed for that purpose by the presbytery, or one of the same presbytery invited by the session, in consultation with presbytery's committee on ministerial relations, to preside on a particular occasion.* [G. XI, 4.] In any emergency, either the moderator appointed by presbytery or the chairman of presbytery's committee on ministerial relations should be consulted by the clerk of session. (See G. XXII, 3.)

c. It should be noted that the moderator of the session must always be a member of the same presbytery with the exception that a minister, employed by two or more presbyteries to labor among their vacant churches, may perform this duty as well as other pastoral duties in a presbytery of which he is not a member, but this only upon specific or general authorization of that presbytery. (See G. XII, 13.)

d. *In congregations where there are two or more pastors (not associate pastors even though installed, or assistant pastors), they shall, when present, alternately preside in the session.* [G. XI, 5.] Associate or assistant pastors may preside only if requested under the conditions noted in a, above; or if appointed by presbytery in cases where they are retained when churches are without pastors. (See G. XX, 1, d.)

4. The clerk and the record. *Every judicatory shall elect a stated clerk whose term of office shall be determined by the judicatory. He shall perform such duties as the electing judicatory may assign, including the recording of their transactions. It shall be the duty of the stated clerk, besides recording the transactions, to preserve the records*

carefully; and to grant extracts from them, whenever properly required; and such extracts, under the hand of the stated clerk, shall be considered as authentic vouchers of the fact which they declare, in any ecclesiastical judicatory, and to every part of the Church. [G. XXVI.]

It should be noted that although the clerk is usually a member of the session, a session may choose its clerk from among the members of the congregation. In such case, the clerk has neither voice nor vote in the proceedings.

See Appendix H (p. 131) for rules for session minutes.

Normally the record of a session meeting contains nothing of general discussion, but only of acts performed and actions taken. The record of attendance should include the names of those present, those excused, and those absent. In any case, the roll must indicate clearly that a quorum was present. The record should note that the meeting was opened and closed with prayer (see G. XI, 11) and that the minutes of the previous meeting were read and approved. (See Appendix C for suggested docket.) At a session meeting convened immediately after a church service, it is not necessary to have an opening prayer.

5. Voting by proxy is not allowed. (See G. V, 4.)

6. The meetings of the sessions should be conducted according to the rules for judicatories adopted by the General Assembly of The United Presbyterian Church in the United States of America, so far as they apply, and, when they do not apply, according to the usual legislative rules of order. (See Appendix G, for General Rules for Judicatories.)

7. Meetings of the session are not open either to the public or to members of the congregation, except by invitation. Neither are the records public. If the clerk is in doubt as to whether he is to grant an extract from the

record as required in 4, above, he should consult the session to secure its decision in the matter. (See G. & W. (U), 46 (3) 52; Dig., p. A862.)

8. In the required rotation of session membership, the provision of the Constitution for communicant members on session committees (see G. XI, 8) may enable the retention of inactive ruling elders on particular committees where their aptitude or talent is needed. Another suggestion based upon the same provision is a Church Officers' Reserve Board, into which may be called not only inactive ruling elders but prospective church officers for training.

B. THE AUTHORITY AND RESPONSIBILITY OF THE SESSION

In general the session is responsible for the whole life of a particular Presbyterian church. Its authority, under the Constitution, is limited only by the Constitution, by the reserved rights of the congregation listed beginning on page 25 of this manual, by the rights of review and control delegated to the presbytery under the Constitution (see p. 49, this chapter), by the authority of the pastor under the Constitution (see Chapter VII of this manual), and finally by limitations which may be inherent in the civil laws governing religious corporations of a particular state. The general charter of the powers and responsibilities of the session is found in the Constitution as follows:

The session is charged with maintaining the spiritual government of the congregation, for which purpose it has power to inquire into the knowledge and Christian conduct of the members of the church; to call before it offenders and witnesses, being members of its own congregation, and to introduce other witnesses, where it may be necessary to bring the process to issue, and when they can be procured to attend; to instruct parents who are communicants to present their children for baptism; to decide who shall be members of the church, and to receive them into the communion of the church upon profession of faith in Jesus Christ, upon presentation of satisfactory certificate of church membership, or, in the absence of such certificate upon the part of persons coming from other churches, upon reaffirmation of faith in Jesus Christ; to grant certificates of dismissal to other churches, which when given to parents shall always include the names of their baptized children; to admonish, to rebuke, to suspend or exclude from the sacraments those who are found to deserve censure; to concert the best measures for promoting the spiritual interests of the congregation; to supervise the church school, the work of the deacons and the trustees, and all the societies or agencies of the congregation; to participate with the minister in the examination, ordination, and installation of ruling elders and deacons on their election by the congregation; and to appoint representatives to higher judicatories of the Church.

Subject to the provisions of the Directory for Worship, the session shall have and exercise exclusive authority over the worship of the congregation, including the musical service; and shall determine the times and places of preaching the Word and all other religious services. It shall also have exclusive authority over the uses to which the church buildings and properties may be put, but may temporarily delegate the determination of such uses, subject always to the superior authority and direction of the session.

A church, if it so desires, may lodge all of the administrative responsibility, both spiritual and corporate, in one body, which shall be the session.

The church session shall have authority over all of the affairs and activities of the particular church, except such matters as may, by this Form of Government, be specifically accorded to the pastor, to the congregation, or to a higher judicatory. The session may from time to time *delegate administrative responsibilities in respect to the care and management of church properties and in respect to the financial affairs of the church either to the board of trustees or to the board of deacons or in part to one and in part to the other, subject always to the superior authority and direction of the session. It may add communicant members to any of its committees and may set up special committees of communicant members responsible to it.*

Should any difference arise between the session and any board or organization of a particular church, it shall be incumbent upon each of them to consider the views of the other with care and respect, earnestly endeavoring to arrive at a conclusion agreeable to both. If they are unable so to do, then the position of the session, as the body having superior responsibility for the welfare and program of the church, shall prevail unless reversed or modified by a higher judicatory.

The worship of God by offerings shall also be under the authority of the session, which shall authorize such offerings for purposes of benevolence as shall by it be deemed wise, with due regard to benevolence budgets and policies recommended by higher judicatories. It is their duty also to develop the grace of liberality in the members of the church. This duty may be performed by the session itself or by specific assignment to the deacons, or to such other body in the church as it deems wise. The offerings received shall be apportioned among the agencies of the Church and among other objects of Christian benevolence, under the supervision of the church session, in such proportion and on such general plan as may from time to time be determined; but the specific designation by the giver of any offering to any cause or causes shall always be respected and the will of the donor carefully carried out. The offerings of the church school and of all the societies or agencies of the church shall be reported regularly to the session of the church for approval. [G. XI, 6–10.]

It will be seen from the above that these powers and responsibilities are exercised in three main relationships: to the presbytery, to all the other bodies within the particular church, including the organized congregation itself, and to the individual members of the congregation.

1. Relationship to the presbytery. A session should recognize clearly that it is responsible to lead and govern the church under its charge so that it may be as effective a Presbyterian church as God in his grace and providence through its efforts will make it. The members of a church session, including all the ruling elders and the ministers, have taken ordination vows (see G. XVII, 7, and XIX, 4) which bind them individually and collectively to try to fulfill this responsibility. Once elders are elected, ordained, and installed, their chief responsibility is toward the presbytery, which supervises and reviews their actions, rather than toward the congregation, which has elected them. This does not mean that a session should be insensible to the wishes of a majority of the congregation (elders may find others elected in their places if they ignore such wishes), but it does mean that a session is responsible to the presbytery to lead the people to support a Presbyterian program of worship, education, fellowship, and benevolence as developed by the Church as a whole and transmitted to the particular church by the presbytery.

Since the presbytery is made up of all the ministers in an area (usually a county or several counties in size) plus a ruling elder elected by the session of each church in the area, the session should realize that the presbytery (which in our form of government is collectively the supervising bishop) is not alien to the particular church. The session of each particular church is as responsible as every other session in the area to determine what kind of presbytery it will be that will supervise its life and work. The aim here, as in all Presbyterian government, is to develop the maximum of responsible freedom.

The specific duties of the session in relationship to the presbytery are as follows:

a. To appoint an elder commissioner to attend each meeting of presbytery, and to encourage this delegate to participate fully in the work and deliberations of the presbytery and to report back to the session (with the pastor) all actions and recommendations of the presbytery which impinge upon the life and program of the particular church.

It should be noted here that when there is more than one installed pastor (not assistant) in a particular church, the session should appoint ruling elder commissioners to the presbytery equal to the number of such pastors. (See G. XII, 3.) When a church is without a pastor, the session has nevertheless the responsibility to be represented in presbytery by one ruling elder.

b. To encourage the pastor and all other ordained ministers as well as commissioned church workers on the staff of the church to attend presbytery and be active in its work.

c. Annually to see that sufficient money is budgeted, raised, and paid promptly from the current expense funds of the church to meet the per capita apportionment determined by presbytery in order that the whole governmental structure of the Presbyterian Church may be supported.

d. Annually to submit its minutes to the presbytery for review and approval.

e. Annually to report to the stated clerk of presbytery, on the statistical forms provided for the purpose, the information requested concerning the life and activity of the church. It is important that there be a stated or special meeting of the session as soon as possible after January 1 each year to approve this report. It should be noted that this report is the report of the session and does not require approval by the congregation.

f. To respond to the benevolence requests of the presbytery for the work of the Presbyterian Church at home and abroad by considering how best the particular church can meet its fair share of the whole program as approved by the presbytery. The minimum response requisite is that the session shall give to the people opportunity to contribute by regular gifts or special offerings, or both, to the worldwide program of the Presbyterian Church. For the specific responsibilities of the session in relation to the benevolence budgets of higher judicatories, the development of stewardship, and the apportionment of all offerings of the congregation and all societies and agencies of the church, see Section 10 of Form of Government, Chapter XI, quoted on page 48 of this manual.

g. To keep the following rolls and such others as may be required from time to time by the presbytery or the General Assembly (see G. XI, 13):

(1) All communicant members in good and regular standing.

(2) All suspended members. (See p. 61, this chapter.)

(3) All children of the Covenant, with dates of births and names of parents. (Optional.)

(4) All baptized children of communicant members.

(5) All affiliated members. (See p. 56, this chapter.)

(6) All nonmembers who are regular contributors to the support of the church.

h. To keep the following records and such others as may be from time to time required by the presbytery or the General Assembly (see G. XI, 13):

(1) Infant baptisms, including names of parents and the birth date of child.

(2) Adult baptisms.

(3) Marriages performed by the pastor and other ministers on the church staff. Also, to include in the record marriages of church members performed by Pres-

byterian ministers other than the above.   (See W. XIV, 9.)

(4) Deaths and other removals from the rolls of the church.

j. To take all actions directed by presbytery or a regularly elected commission thereof, unless the session formally votes to complain of the action to the synod. For the way in which such a complaint may be initiated and followed, the session must consult *Presbyterian Law for the Presbytery* and the Constitution itself.

A session should realize that the powers of the presbytery are great enough to determine that a regularly elected session may even be dismissed by presbytery and a committee of the presbytery put in its place to govern the congregation if and when in the considered judgment of the presbytery a session is unable or unwilling to perform its duties to the whole Church as outlined above. The session's freedom and discretion are real and wide. There are, however, limits of which the presbytery is the judge. It should be remembered that Presbyterian freedom is responsible freedom.

2. Relationships to other bodies within the particular church.

From the Constitutional provisions quoted at the beginning of section B of this chapter, it is clear that all the other boards, agencies, and activities within a particular Presbyterian church are subject to the ultimate control of the session.   (See also G. XXVIII.)   In this manual, Chapter VI contains the specific law and relationship to the trustees. Chapter II records the rights and duties of the congregation itself and the session's relationship to the congregation. Chapter V treats similarly the relationship to the board of deacons. Here, therefore, will be treated only the relationship between the session and all other societies and organizations that may be from time to time established within a particular church. The most important of these are usually the church school, including young people's organizations and adult classes, the men's and women's organizations or societies, and the young adult organizations.

In general the session is responsible for supervising and directing all these organizations to the end that the church may grow and flourish. Depending upon the size of the church and of the session and upon the session's competence and desire, the authority to carry on these programs and organizations may be delegated to others or exerted directly through committees of the session. It should be clear that no organization within a particular church is or can be independent of the session. When the session delegates its authority to any group within the church to carry on any program or activity whatever, that group must report at least annually to the session and secure approval of its program activities and its budgets, both of expense and benevolence. (See G. XXVIII.)

Here again a wise session will try in the Presbyterian way to give the maximum amount of responsible freedom. But the session cannot neglect its own responsibility to guide the whole church in all its parts toward the fulfillment of the Presbyterian Church's program, as developed by the Church as a whole and received by the session through the presbytery.

When the officers or members of any organization or society within the particular church resist the session as it tries to exert its proper authority, the Constitution provides that the position of the session shall prevail. (See G. XI, 9.) In addition, such members risk the discipline of the session as outlined beginning on p. 60 in the following section.

3. The relationship of the session to the individual members of the congregation. In a Presbyterian church, mem-

bers are received into the church and dismissed from the church by the session and are subject to its discipline so long as they are members.

a. How communicant members are received into the church.

(1) Baptized children of members are received into full communicant membership of the church by vote of the session when in the judgment of the session they have reached years of discretion, have been *examined . . . as to their knowledge and piety*, and have made profession of faith in and promise of obedience to the Lord Jesus Christ. Ordinarily a further profession of faith is made publicly in the presence of the congregation. (See W. IX, 2, 3.)

It is the duty of the session toward these *children, born within the pale of the visible Church, and dedicated to God in baptism*, to see that they are taught the Christian faith, *to pray, to abhor sin, to love God, and to obey and serve the Lord Jesus Christ. And when* [in the judgment of the session] *they come to years of discretion they should be earnestly reminded that they are members of the Church by birthright and that it is their duty and privilege personally to accept Christ as Savior and Lord, to confess him before men, and seek admission to the Lord's Supper.* [W. IX, 1.]

(2) Unbaptized persons are received into the church by vote of the session upon their profession of faith in Christ and their promise of obedience to him. This is followed by baptism in the name of the Father, and of the Son, and of the Holy Spirit. (See W. VIII, 5; G. &. W. (U), 15, 366; Dig., p. A256.) It is clear that the reception into membership of The United Presbyterian Church in the United States of America is reception into the Church of Christ as a whole. For this reason it is not proper for a session to require more than the steps enumerated above from any person sincerely desiring membership, although the session may require attendance at such

classes as it sets up and the undergoing of an examination as to Christian knowledge satisfactory to itself before accepting a profession of faith and also a promise of obedience.

(3) Communicant members who are in good standing in other particular Presbyterian churches or in other Christian Churches which recognize The United Presbyterian Church in the United States of America as a part of the one catholic Church of Christ are ordinarily received into the membership of a particular Presbyterian church by letter of transfer on vote of the session.

It is largely left to the discretion of the session as to what church letters it will receive. (See W. IX, 4; G. & W. (U), 120; Dig., p. A261; Hist. Dig. (P), 1373 ff.) A session does not have to give its reason for refusing to receive a member of another particular Presbyterian church, much less from another denomination.

The ordinary rule to govern sessions would be to receive on letter of transfer a member of any Church with which we are officially in correspondence through the World Alliance of Reformed Churches Holding the Presbyterian Order, the World Council of Churches, and the National Council of the Churches of Christ in the United States of America, plus such other Christian Churches as, in the judgment of the session, are not heretical or schismatic. From time to time the General Assembly has indicated that letters should not be received from such groups as the Christian Science Church, the Universalist or Unitarian Churches.

A session may require prospective members coming from other Presbyterian Churches and from other Christian Churches to attend classes of instruction and to undergo an examination as to their Christian knowledge satisfactory to itself.

(4) Persons who have been baptized, but who are not communicant members in good standing and so are

not covered by (3) above, or who cannot for other reason secure church letters of transfer, may be received into the membership of the church either on profession of faith and promise of obedience to Christ or on the reaffirmation of that faith and a new promise of obedience as the case may be. The following cases are suggested as illustrative, if not exhaustive:

(a) A baptized communicant member who is not in good standing may be received by vote of the session on reaffirmation of faith. This action should be taken only after writing to the session under whose jurisdiction he is, asking it to restore him and issue a letter of transfer.

(b) A baptized Roman Catholic may be received either on profession of faith or on reaffirmation of faith. Discretion is left to the session as to the mode of reception, even to the inclusion of a rebaptism, if it is desired by the new member, although a session should be careful not to require rebaptism of anyone who has already been baptized in the name of the Triune God.

(c) A baptized member of a church or a denomination which will not grant a letter to a Presbyterian church should ordinarily be received on the reaffirmation of his faith.

(d) A baptized but unconfirmed Episcopalian, Lutheran, etc., may be received on profession of faith as under (1) above.

A session should take care to notify the last church in which a member being received on reaffirmation of faith has held membership so that the person's name may not appear in the membership of two churches and so that in the case of one coming from the membership of a particular Presbyterian church it may not inadvertently place in good standing a member under discipline by another session.

b. Affiliated members. *When any member removes*

from a community in which the church of which he is a member is located, for the purpose of securing an education or serving in the Armed Forces of our nation, or in any other national or state service which precludes the establishment of local legal residence, the session of said church may issue to him a certificate of good standing, which, if issued, shall be used by the member receiving it solely for the purpose of establishing affiliated membership, without enrolling as a regular member, in a church located in the community of which the educational institution he attends is a part or adjacent to the post to which he is assigned, or in the community of temporary residence. The certificate shall be good for two years, subject to renewal. The session issuing the certificate shall duly certify the fact to the pastor of the church named therein, and shall retain the name of the member on the roll of the home church. [D. II, 2 (a).]

When any member resides in a community outside the United States, either as a lay missionary or fraternal worker, or in a secular capacity, and desires to establish an affiliated relationship with a congregation belonging to a Church which is in correspondence with the General Assembly, the session of the church of which he is a member may, at his request, issue a certificate of good standing permitting him to establish affiliated membership with the said congregation during the period of his residence in the community. The certificate should be good for two years, subject to renewal. The session issuing the certificate shall duly certify the fact to the pastor of the church named therein, and shall retain the name of the member on the roll of the home church. [D. II, 2(b)] (This will go into effect at the time of the meeting of the General Assembly in 1959.)

c. How members may be released from their obligations assumed when they became members. Perhaps the most difficult part of Presbyterian law for the average modern

American Presbyterian to understand is that which applies to the obligation of membership in the church. Since to become a member is a free and voluntary act, it is hard for many to understand why it is sometimes so difficult to free oneself from the obligation accepted at membership. The Presbyterian Church is not a club from which one can freely resign, for under some conditions such a resignation would be in the Church viewpoint the equivalent of renouncing God and repudiating the Lord Jesus Christ. The session of a particular Presbyterian church is, therefore, bound by its Constitutional obligations to do all within its power to keep every member on the roll of that church as an active worshiping Christian. There are many easy ways to change one's membership from one particular church to another. It is easy to become a member of another Christian church or even of another religion entirely. But so long as a member is alive and has not formally removed himself from the care and discipline of the session of his church by joining another, he cannot finally be free of the church which once he voluntarily joined.

With this general understanding in mind, the following list of ways by which a member can be finally released by a session from his obligations to a particular Presbyterian church will be more easily understood.

(1) The name may be removed from the roll by the session upon knowledge or notification of the member's death.

(2) The name may be finally removed from the roll when, upon application of the member, a letter of transfer has been granted by the session to another particular Presbyterian church or to a church of another denomination, and notice has come that the member has been received by that church.

Letters of transfer must always be given to a particular church, never in general, and should be granted by a session whenever requested by a member to such churches only as are suggested in section 3, a (3), above. If, however, a member indicates his intention to join a church to which the session cannot grant a letter of transfer, the session may as a matter of courtesy issue a statement of his good standing. His name would then be removed from the roll under the provisions of (3), below.

The session . . . has power . . . to grant certificates of dismissal to other churches, which when given to parents shall always include the names of their baptized children. [G. XI, 6.]

(3) *If a church member renounces the communion of the Church by joining any other religious body, without a regular dismission, although such conduct is disorderly, the session shall take no other action in the case than record the fact, and order his name to be erased from the roll.* [D. VII, 2 (a), par. 1.]

(4) *When a church member against whom no charges are pending shall inform the session that he is fully persuaded that he has no right to come to the Lord's Table, the session shall confer with him on the subject, and may, should he continue of the same mind, and his attendance on the other means of grace be regular, excuse him from attendance on the Lord's Supper; and, after fully satisfying themselves that his judgment is not the result of mistaken views, shall erase his name from the roll of communicants, and make record of their action in the case.* [D. VII, 2 (a), par. 1.]

(5) *When a church member so removes from the bounds of the particular church of which he is a member that the session is unable after due and diligent search to ascertain his place of residence, the session may erase his name, after two years of such absence, from the roll of active communicant members of the church. The session may restore an erased name to the roll of communicant members whenever fully satisfied that such action is justified.* [D. VII, 2 (a), par. 2.]

(6) When a member of the church is ordained to the gospel ministry by the presbytery, the fact shall be noted and the name erased from the roll. ("Erasure" in this and other references is a technical term and does not imply that the name should be rubbed out.)

(7) A name may be erased from the roll when in due process a member has been tried according to judicial discipline and the ultimate degree of church censure, excommunication, has been determined by the session and the judgment has been pronounced. (See section d, below, for the processes of judicial discipline.)

It will be noted that no one of the above methods is designed to handle the situation, unfortunately too prevalent, when members just drift away, failing to attend or support the church, but do not take any decisive act which allows a session to apply one of the seven final actions listed above. It is worth repeating that a mere resignation does not release the session from its obligation to continue to try to win back the disaffected member. This situation must be handled by some process of discipline, as explained below.

d. The discipline of church members by the session:

"Discipline" is used here in a technical sense, meaning the responsible oversight of the membership of a particular church to the end that no member by his acts or words may be able with impunity to bring shame upon the Lord Jesus Christ or to wander from his way without loving admonition and all effort to keep him an active member in the worship and fellowship of the church.

The session is charged with maintaining the spiritual government of the congregation, for which purpose it has power to inquire into the knowledge and Christian conduct of the members of the church; to call before it offenders and witnesses, being members of its own congregation, and to introduce other witnesses, where it may be necessary to bring the process to issue, and when they can

*be procured to attend; . . . to admonish, to rebuke, to
suspend or exclude from the sacraments those who are
found to deserve censure.* [G. XI, 6.] Remembering that
the above powers are, as all church powers, *only ministerial and declarative* [G. I, 7], and are intended to be
used only when the members themselves really feel a part
of the church and want to remain in good standing within
it, one can see why in this secular age sessions rarely conduct any sort of trial of church members even though the
actions and words of members bring shame and disgrace
upon the church and the Lord Jesus Christ.

A session should remember that it has these powers and
should be prepared to use them if ever necessary. But it
will be usually found that when a delinquent or rebellious
or contumacious member realizes that a trial may be held,
he will in some way renounce the church so that the trial
need not take place.

No session should begin a trial without a careful study
of the Book of Discipline of the latest date, and since in
these days there are few trials at the session level in our
Church, this manual makes no attempt to cover the rather
complicated legal procedures of judicial discipline, which
procedures are designed fully to protect the rights of each
church member as well as to uphold the honor of the Lord
Jesus Christ and to maintain the purity of the Church.
(See D. I, 6. See also *Presbyterian Law for the Presbytery.*)

In order to handle the too prevalent cases in which
members drift away from the church, the following two
rules have been recently revised in the Constitution:

(1) *A person whose name has been on the roll of
nonresident church members* [see previous paragraph of
this section of the Book of Discipline] *for a period of two
years, and whose address is known, shall be again advised
by the session of the church of which he is a member to
apply for a regular certificate of dismission, and failing to
do so, he may, without further notice, be suspended from*

*the communion of the Church until he shall satisfy the
session of the propriety of his restoration.* [D. VII, 3, d.]

(2) *Any resident church member who shall per-
sistently absent himself from the ordinances of the
church for two years in a manner to be regarded as a
serious injury to the cause of religion may, after diligent
effort has been made by the session to restore him to
active fulfillment of his membership, and he has been duly
notified of its intention, be suspended from the communion of the Church until he shall satisfy the session of
the propriety of his restoration.* [D. VII, 4.]

It must be remembered that members so suspended are
still members of the church and subject to the discipline
of the session. The session is required to keep their names
upon a separate roll of suspended members. As noted
above, they may in the discretion of the session be re-
stored to the active roll by simple majority vote.

The heart of the matter is that a session may suspend
members only if every possible effort has been made to
avoid the necessity. With regard to the general responsibility of each session, the Form of Government requires:

*Every session shall keep registers or rolls of persons ad-
mitted to or suspended from the Lord's Table; and of the
deaths and other removals of church members, but the
names of members shall be placed upon or removed from
the rolls of the church only by order of the session, and
in accordance with the provisions of the Book of Discipline.* [G. XI, 13.] The minister and ruling elders have
a special and continuing Constitutional duty to church
members: *Ministers and ruling elders of the Church
should frequently visit the families and members of the
flock over which the Holy Spirit has made them overseers;
to pray with, instruct, comfort, encourage, and admonish
the people, especially in times of unusual affliction or
temptation, to assist them in the study of the Scriptures
and doctrinal standards of the Church, and to stimulate*

them to family religion and fidelity in all Christian duty.
[W. XV, 1.]

Quite often after a member has been suspended (particularly in the case of nonresidents) a request comes to the session for a letter of transfer. Such letter may be granted only after a vote has been taken to restore such suspended member to the active roll. Courtesy to other churches and the responsibility of the session to try any means to restore a suspended member to active Christian life suggest that a session should, whenever requested, take this action and also send with the letter of transfer a note indicating for how long a period the member in question has been inactive and on the suspended roll.

The actual power of a session to guide the life of a particular Presbyterian church depends to a great measure on its power, under the Constitution, over the membership of the church. Although a session must be careful not to be arbitrary in the use of this power, the opposite danger is much more prevalent in the church: sessions too often allow disloyal and scandalous behavior on the part of members to rend the church and ruin its effectiveness. The session is responsible for seeing that this does not happen.

4. Relationship to the particular churches of other denominations. Co-operation with other particular churches in evangelism, weekday church schools, and other community enterprises has long been the custom throughout the Church. To the first of the Preliminary Principles of our Constitution, quoted on page 15 of this manual, there has been added what is in effect a practical footnote. *Communions and particular churches ought to co-operate in so far as possible in giving expression to their oneness in Jesus Christ within his body, the ecumenical, catholic Church.* [G. III, 5.] The session has the primary responsibility for such co-operation.

THE DUTIES AND RIGHTS OF THE BOARD OF DEACONS

1. It is part of our faith that Christians *are bound to maintain an holy fellowship and communion . . . in relieving each other in outward things, according to their several abilities and necessities.* [C. XXVI, 2.]

To fulfill this obligation, following the pattern of the early church, the Constitution provides that any particular church desiring to do so may have a board of deacons which *shall minister to those in need, to the sick, to the friendless, and to any who may be in distress, in accordance with the Scriptural duties of the office. There may be delegated to the board of deacons, under the direction of the session, certain specifically designated responsibilities relating to the development of the grace of liberality in the members of the church, to the devising of effective methods of collecting the gifts of the people, to the finances and properties of the church, and to its evangelistic, missionary, and educational programs. The board of deacons shall assume such duties, not limited to the foregoing, as may be delegated to it by the session.* [G. X, 5.]

The Scriptures clearly point out deacons as distinct officers in the Church. The office is one of sympathy and service, after the example of the Lord Jesus.

To the office of deacon should be chosen persons of spiritual mind, exemplary life, friendly spirit, and sound judgment. [G. X, 1-2.]

2. When the congregation so desires, the church may constitute a board of deacons. The board of deacons shall consist of the pastor (or co-pastors) of the congregation and its deacons in active service. When, however, more than one minister serves a church, the session may name annually, with the consent of the pastor, one or more of these ministers to membership on the board of deacons in place of the pastor or in addition to him. [G. X, 3.]

3. The pastor, if a member of the board of deacons, shall be its moderator, except as hereinafter provided. With the consent of the pastor, whether or not he is a member of the board, the session may: (1) designate as moderator of the board any other minister who has been named to membership thereon; or (2) authorize the board to elect a moderator from its membership. The board of deacons may also elect from its membership a vice-moderator, a secretary, and a treasurer of the funds of the board. [G. X, 6.]

4. Of this board, three members, if there be so many, shall be necessary to constitute a quorum, unless the board numbers more than nine, when one third of the board shall be necessary to constitute a quorum. [G. X, 4.]

It will be noted that although a session cannot complete a quorum for legal or formal action without the pastor or some other minister of the presbytery present, the board of deacons may have a quorum constituted entirely of deacons.

5. The board shall hold stated meetings. Special meetings shall be held whenever requested by two of its members or by the session or by the pastor. The board shall keep a record of its proceedings, and of all funds at its disposal and their distribution, and shall submit its records

to the session for approval at least once a year, and at other times upon the request of the session. [G. X, 7.]

6. If it is desired by the session and the congregation, it is proper and possible for the deacons to be elected the trustees of the church and to be entrusted by the session with the care and management of the temporalities of the church. (See G. X, 5, quoted as part of paragraph 1, above. See also G. & W. (U), 40; Hist. Dig. (U), Ch. XL; Dig., p. A238.)

7. A session may wish to delegate to the board of deacons any of its spiritual services to the congregation which it cannot fully and satisfactorily do itself, including such activities as calling upon the sick, visitation, evangelism, and even the serving of the Communion. (See G. X, 5, quoted above. (See also G. & W. (U), 40; Dig., p. A239.) But deacons may not represent the church in the higher judicatories. (See G. & W. (U), 37; Dig., p. A239.)

8. Both men and women are eligible to this office; and a church, if it so desires, may have a whole board of women deacons. Formerly (see G. XIII, 8 (P)), deaconesses apart from the board of deacons were authorized. Also previously, a deaconess who had pursued a course of instruction and had been set apart by the presbytery might serve as an employee of a particular church. (See Dig. p. A762.) Such workers are now ordinarily termed commissioned church workers. For the Constitutional provisions in relation to commissioned church workers, see Form of Government, Chapter XXIII. See also Chapter VIII, B, 5, in this manual.

VI

THE DUTIES AND RIGHTS OF THE BOARD OF TRUSTEES

Although most Presbyterian churches carry on harmoniously in spite of a rather hazy understanding of the distinction between the rights and duties of the session on the one hand and the rights and duties of the board of trustees on the other, nevertheless it is the relation between these two bodies that produces a very high percentage of the misunderstandings that occur in the particular Presbyterian church.

The beginning of the difficulty goes back very early in American church history when, because in colonial days the Presbyterian Church belonged to the unrecognized and dissenting religious groups, it was necessary for it to hold its property by the legal dodge of establishing a corporation with private individuals as trustees who were only indirectly responsible to the governing body of the Church. If that had not been so, doubtless our Church would have followed the Scottish practice of having the management of its financial and business affairs vested in the deacons, who are clearly under the direction and control of the session in any Presbyterian church.

But whatever the historical reasons for it, the fact is that particular Presbyterian churches are troubled by the present situation in which clearly the session is the responsible body under church law for all that goes on in them, while there is a board of trustees which under civil law appears to have quite independent power and control over all the church's property and financial affairs.

The very prevalent idea that the session is limited to spiritual leadership, while the trustees control the temporal affairs of the church (see G. XI, 6 and also G. XXXII, 7), is not a completely satisfactory answer. When a close point is at issue, who is to decide what is spiritual and what is temporal? The Constitution has been recently amended to make clear that trustees' duties are essentially corporate duties and not temporal.

From the point of view of Presbyterian Church law, again and again in crucial cases supported by decisions of state and Federal courts, it is clear that the session is the supreme governing body in a particular Presbyterian church. This does not mean, however, that sessions can do whatever they please and that trustees are reduced to rubber stamps. Rather it means that a situation of checks and balances is found here as in many other places in Presbyterian law. Presbytery and General Assembly, session and congregation, pastor and ruling elders—all these as well as session and trustees are set against one another with certain duties and rights limiting the duties and rights of the other.

Boards of trustees then must realize that their position is not, as they so easily grow to think, that of the directors of a business corporation. The very name trustee should remind them that the property they hold is in trust not merely for the particular church corporation and its purposes, but for The United Presbyterian Church in the United States of America; and that this Presbyterian Church is a Church with a being and a law of its own. It would be out of place in such a manual as this to marshal from both ecclesiastical and civil law the arguments for the position taken in this chapter. The Presbyterian Digest has the essential material bearing upon this question. Here it is sufficient to quote from the Form of Government:

The radical principles of Presbyterian Church government and discipline are: That the several different congregations of believers, taken collectively, constitute one Church of Christ, called emphatically the Church; that a larger part of the Church, or a representation of it, should govern a smaller, or determine matters of controversy which arise therein; that, in like manner, a representation of the whole should govern and determine in regard to every part, and to all the parts united: that is, that a majority shall govern; and consequently that appeals may be carried from lower to higher judicatories, till they be finally decided by the collected wisdom and united voice of the whole Church. [G. V, 1.]

The duties and rights of boards of trustees in a particular Presbyterian church must then be understood primarily within the framework of the whole Constitutional law of the Presbyterian Church and secondarily within the jurisdiction of the civil law of the state. The pertinent sections of the state law governing religious corporations, the provisions of the articles of incorporation or charter of the particular church corporation, and the provisions of the bylaws of the particular church corporation (see Appendix B of this manual for model bylaws of a particular church corporation) must be available for the guidance of all trustees in the performance of their duties. It will be found, however, that these provisions stemming out of the civil law seldom give to a board of trustees any extra powers as against the session. More often their force is to limit the authority of the trustees by the rights of the particular church corporation and the rights of the members thereof.

It would be unfortunate for trustees to suppose from the above that their power and authority was so much restricted that the office was hardly worth the attention of able men. The duties and rights of boards of trustees, as outlined below, should dispel any such idea.

A. DUTIES

1. *Each particular church, except in states forbidding the incorporation of religious bodies, shall cause a corporation to be formed to receive, hold, manage, and transfer property, and to facilitate the management of its corporate affairs in such a manner as may be directed by the particular church from time to time, in conformity with the Constitution of The United Presbyterian Church in the United States of America.*

A particular church which is not incorporated should select from among its membership trustees who shall have the power and authority to receive, hold, manage, and transfer property, and to facilitate the management of its civil affairs in such manner as may be directed by the particular church from time to time, in conformity with the Constitution of The United Presbyterian Church in the United States of America. [G. XXXII, 4-5.]

The trustees are the responsible officers of such corporations, and their duties are therefore in general to govern the affairs of the corporation to the best interests not only of the particular church but also of The United Presbyterian Church in the United States of America. (See G. XXXII, 8, quoted under Chapter III, C, of this manual.)

2. The duties and responsibilities of trustees are defined in the Constitution as follows:

Whether by civil law the trustees of a particular church hold title to its property or are the officers of a corporation which holds title thereto, they shall deal with such property only as they may be authorized or directed by the session, and their authority in respect to the selling, mortgaging, and leasing of real property shall be subject also to any rights reserved to the congregation by civil law or the bylaws of the particular church and to the permission of presbytery as herein provided.

The trustees of a particular church shall exercise any other powers or authorities vested in them by civil law in conformity with the actions of the session as conveyed to them from time to time. They shall also perform such other duties relating to the property or finances of the church as may be delegated to them by the session. The trustees shall submit a financial statement of all matters committed to them and a report of their proceedings to the session for review at least once a year and at other times upon request of the session.

While trustees, like other boards and bodies of a particular church, hold authority subordinate to that of the session, the office of trustee is one of dignity and responsibility, requiring ability and devotion. Trustees, upon their election, shall be properly recognized at a service of worship and set apart to the discharge of their responsibility by prayer. [G. XXXII, 9.]

These duties and responsibilities may be enumerated thus:

a. To hold title (either as the corporation (see G. XXXII, 5) or for the corporation (see G. XXXII, 4)) to all the property of the particular church including the land and buildings for church use.

b. To keep in repair the property used for purposes of the church program as determined by the session and congregation.

c. To invest all funds given or bequeathed to the church for endowment (if any), paying particular attention to the terms of the gift or bequest as to any specification of the use of the income. If there are no specific directions, it is the duty of the trustees to ascertain from the session and congregation the will of the church as to the use of the income. Depending upon the bylaws and the customs of the particular church with regard to the forming of its annual budget (see f, below), trustees may have more or less power of direction or recommendation in this regard.

d. To supervise the management of all other property which it holds.

e. To protect the properties of the church with sufficient insurance coverage (liability, theft, fire, etc.).

f. To develop under the direction of or in co-operation with the session the annual budget for the current expenses of the congregation, if this responsibility (as is usual) has been delegated to them by resolution of the session or according to the custom of the particular church.

The best procedure for establishing the annual budget of a particular church is to entrust to a budget committee, made up of representatives of both session and trustees, with the pastor ex officio a member, the task of forming a total budget of income from all sources and expenditures for all causes (the local and general mission). When such a budget has been prepared by the committee, having regard to the whole program of the Church, which program is the responsibility of the session, and having regard to the financial stability of the corporation, which is the responsibility of the trustees, it should be submitted as a whole to both session and trustees for approval. If both approve, it is the best procedure for the budget as a whole to be submitted to the congregation for its approval. Corporation approval of the budget is required in many churches by state law, or by charter or bylaws, and it is good practice in any case.

If either the trustees or the session disapproves the budget as first submitted by the budget committee, an attempt should be made by negotiation to reconcile or compromise the disagreement, using the device of a meeting of the elders and trustees together, if such method appears wise or necessary.

If the differences cannot be reconciled between the two boards, a full report of the disagreement and the reasons therefor should be made to the congregation, which should then choose between the budgets offered, or decide upon a compromise between them.

In all such disagreements, the trustees should remember that the session is responsible to the presbytery for carrying out an adequate Presbyterian program in the church, and the session should realize that the trustees are responsible for keeping the church corporation able to meet its obligations and pay its bills. A spirit of fair play and an attempt on the part of all to understand the point of view of those who differ should, with the above procedure, avoid dangerous divisions over the budget.

The above procedure is suggested as the best way to preserve to the session its proper authority over the whole program of the church together with its sole authority over benevolences and church music; and at the same time to preserve to the board of trustees a responsible supervision of the financial affairs of the church corporation.

The solution of any differences between the board of trustees and the session is indicated by the Constitutional provisions relating to all organizations and boards of the church.

Should any difference arise between the session and any board or organization of a particular church, it shall be incumbent upon each of them to consider the views of the other with care and respect, earnestly endeavoring to arrive at a conclusion agreeable to both. If they are unable so to do, then the position of the session, as the body having superior responsibility for the welfare and program of the church, shall prevail unless reversed or modified by a higher judicatory. [G. XI, 9.]

3. To call a meeting of the church corporation when directed by the session or presbytery.

4. When a particular church is dissolved by presbytery, to convey all property to the presbytery. (See G. XXXII, 12.)

5. To follow the directions of a legally called corporation meeting.

B. RIGHTS

The rights of trustees are limited by the Constitution of The United Presbyterian Church in the United States of America and by the laws of the state governing trustees of religious corporations, and by the charter and bylaws of the particular church corporation. In general, however, the rights of the board of trustees are:

1. To receive and hold property. (See G. XXXII, 4, 5, 9.)

2. To transfer property. (See G. XXXII, 4, 5, 9.) This right is, however, strictly limited.
   A particular church shall not sell or mortgage any of its real property without the written permission of the presbytery transmitted through the session of the particular church.
   A particular church shall not lease its real property used for purposes of worship, or lease for more than five years any of its other real property, without the written permission of the presbytery transmitted through the session of the particular church. [G. XXXII, 13.]

3. To handle any of the financial or business affairs of the church delegated to it by the session.

4. To call a meeting of the church corporation.

5. As members of the church to memorialize the presbytery directly or through congregational resolution if in its judgment the session is jeopardizing the financial stability of the particular church corporation.

VII

THE DUTIES AND RIGHTS OF THE PASTOR

The office of the ministry is the first in the Church in both dignity and usefulness. The person who fills this office has, in Scripture, obtained different names expressive of his various duties. As he has the oversight of the flock of Christ he is termed bishop. As he feeds them with spiritual food he is termed pastor. As he serves Christ in the Church he is termed minister. As it is his duty to be grave and prudent, and an example of the flock, and to govern well in the house and Kingdom of Christ, he is termed presbyter or elder. As he is sent to declare the will of God to sinners, and to beseech them to be reconciled to God through Christ, he is termed ambassador. And as he dispenses the manifold grace of God and the ordinances instituted by Christ he is termed steward of the mysteries of God. Both men and women may be called to this office. [G. VIII, 2.]

The antique wording of the above should not obscure from us the fact that it is there that the duties and rights of the pastor are indicated. The duties of the people to their pastor are outlined in Chapter II of this manual.

A. DUTIES

1. The title "pastor" indicates his chief responsibility upon accepting his call, namely, to bring to the people spiritual sustenance and to be the guard of their souls. In

these days it is not wise to press too far the metaphor of shepherd and sheep. Nevertheless, that aspect of it which Christ himself emphasized, the shepherd's interest in and care for each sheep and lamb of his fold, should be singled out as the primary responsibility of a Christian pastor. It has been pointed out that Christianity is the only religion that has developed this kind of ministry in its leadership. Other faiths produce prophets and priests. The pastor, who calls upon the sick, who seeks out the wayward, who concerns himself with all the problems of his people, is a strictly Christian phenomenon.

2. Closely allied to this primary responsibility is a second duty which is indicated by his title of "minister" or "servant." The Form of Government, quoted above, suggests that his primary service is to Jesus Christ. Yet Jesus, who came not to be served but to serve, made it clear in the parable of the last judgment, that service unto his brethren was the way to serve him. A pastor needs therefore to keep high on his list of duties the service not only to his own people, but to all the people of the community to which he is called.

3. His title of "presbyter" or "elder" emphasizes two of the pastor's duties. He is the chief officer of the congregation and must associate himself as moderator of the session with the ruling elders in the government and discipline of the congregation. His duties in church government are not, however, confined to the particular church. He must take his full share in the work of the presbytery, which supervises the life of all the churches in the area; and when appointed, he must respond to the calls upon him of the synod and General Assembly. Pastors and people both need to recognize more fully than often is the case this vital and time-consuming responsibility of the pastor in Presbyterian church government.

4. The second duty that the title of "presbyter" or "elder" indicates is the requirement that the pastor shall *be grave and prudent, and an example to the flock.* [G. VIII, 2.] This responsibility is made even more explicit in the ordination vows which every Presbyterian minister has taken. He has promised to *endeavor by the grace of God to adorn the profession of the gospel in . . . [his] manner of life, and to walk with exemplary piety before the flock of which God shall make . . . [him] overseer.* [G. XIX, 4 (8).]

5. The significance of the pastor's title "ambassador" is in his duty to speak for God to his people and to the community. He is a prophet, finding his message in the Scriptures by the guidance of the Holy Spirit, and should remember that his authority is directly dependent upon the source of his message. His duty to teach his people the will of God and to preach to them the redemptive gospel of Christ as taught in the Scriptures is here emphasized. Again this duty is made explicit in his ordination vow *to be zealous and faithful in maintaining the truths of the gospel.* [G. XIX, 4 (7).]

6. He is further titled *steward of the mysteries of God* [G. VIII, 2], which points to his priestly functions and duties. He is to pray with and for his people. He leads them in the regular services of corporate worship. He administers the sacraments of Baptism and of Holy Communion.

7. Basic to all the above is the duty that is suggested by his title of "bishop" or "overseer" of the particular church. As an ordained Presbyterian minister who has accepted a call by the hands of the presbytery, he is responsible, so far as he is able, for guiding the particular church in its whole life and program so that it shall be a living and effective part of the Church of Jesus Christ and of the

Presbyterian branch thereof. It is the pastor's duty to lead and to admonish so that the particular church for which he is before God responsible shall be and become the best Presbyterian church it can be or become.

It is obvious from the above that no human being can be a perfect pastor. Some men will perform some parts of their duties better than the other parts. He has promised in his ordination *to be faithful and diligent in the exercise of all . . . duties as a Christian and a minister of the gospel, whether personal or relative, private or public.* [G. XIX, 4 (8).] It should be obvious too that most men in such position and responsibility will do better under proper encouragement than under unfair criticism.

B. RIGHTS

The rights of a pastor, as pastor, are few but important.

1. By the installing act of the presbytery he is moderator of the session. Without him present and presiding, the elders are not a session. (See this manual, Chapter IV, p. 43, for exceptions.)

2. Under the Constitution and in harmony with his ordination vows (see G. XIX, 4) he is the judge of what he will preach, how he will conduct worship (see W. II, 1, and III, 3), whose children he will baptize (see C. XXVIII, 4, and Larger Catechism, Q. 166), whom he will marry (see C. XXIV and W. XIV, 2, 3, 5, 7, 10, 11), and how he will fulfill his many responsibilities subject only to the presbytery (see G. XII, 7) and not to the rule of the elders, much less the board of trustees or the congregation. His elders should be his counselors, but he and they need to remember that he is responsible under God and his conscience, not to the particular church of which he is pastor, but to the whole Church through the presbytery, which made him pastor by act of the presbytery.

3. Specific rights are guaranteed to the pastor by the Constitution.

a. He *shall be a member of* the nominating committee of the congregation *ex officio but without vote.* [G. XVII, 1(2).]

b. The members of the congregation in the call of the pastor state: *And we promise and oblige ourselves to review with you the adequacy of this compensation annually, prior to the adoption of the church budget.* [G. XX, 6.] (See G. XXVII, 1.)

In Chapter X of this manual are outlined various procedures that should be followed when there is trouble in a particular church. Both pastor and people should be careful to follow the legal steps whenever a pastor fails in his duties or is deprived of his rights.

VIII

THE DUTIES AND RIGHTS OF THOSE EMPLOYED ON THE STAFF

Since the pastor by virtue of his office is the chief executive officer in any particular church (see Chapter VII of this manual), the other persons employed by the church serve under his direction although not under his authority. Authority in a Presbyterian church is always lodged in ordered groups and is not given to one individual to exercise over another. The pastor must, therefore, counsel with the elders, trustees, or specially appointed committees (such as the music committee or the committee on Christian education) as he exercises his leadership over the other members of a church staff.

With the exception of ordained ministers and commissioned church workers, whose cases will be treated separately below, all members of the church staff are employed by and responsible to the session (in the case of those engaged in the program of the church) or to the trustees (in the case of those engaged in purely temporal work, such as caretakers). In large churches where the staff is numerous, the session may also delegate to the trustees the negotiation and fixing of terms and conditions of employment of all staff members, even of those whose work is of a primarily program nature. But even so, the supervision of all workers in the program must remain ultimately with the session. In smaller churches there are sometimes one or two employed whose duties are such that the session and trustees necessarily divide the supervisory authority (for example, a secretary who keeps the rolls as well as the financial books of the church). All the more in such cases it is clear that the authority must be exercised through the pastor in order to avoid contradictions in the policy of the two boards.

All employees of a church do not necessarily have to be members of the church. There perhaps are situations where it appears to be advantageous if they are not, but they should be interested in and in basic harmony with the purposes and program of the church.

A. DUTIES

1. All employees of a particular church are responsible to the employing body within the church to do the task outlined in the job description (or call) made at the time of employment.

2. All employees owe loyalty to the pastor and to the other members of the church staff.

3. All employees ought to show Christian courtesy to the members of the church and to the public even under trying circumstances, since much of the reputation of a church is in the hands of those employed by it.

4. All employees ought to lead a Christian life, lest their working in the church harm its reputation in the community.

B. RIGHTS

1. Of all persons (including student assistants) who are neither ordained ministers nor commissioned church workers.

    a. Regular payment of salary agreed upon.

b. Customary notice of dismissal or an extra payment of salary in lieu of it.

c. Protection by the pastor or employing body from unreasonable demands for overtime work or for unusual services by members of the congregation or others.

d. A generous and Christian employment policy by the church, including vacation, time off for illness, pension plan, etc. (The church should lead rather than lag in its generous treatment of employees.)

2. Of an ordained minister called as associate pastor.

a. A call by the congregation approved by the presbytery (see G. XX, 1, c), the terms of which may not be changed without action by both the congregation and the presbytery. (See Appendix D, 2.)

b. A service of ordination or installation by the presbytery. (See G. XIX, 4; XX, 12, 13, 14, 15.)

c. Supervision of his work by the session through the pastor.

d. Access to the session to discuss his work. Furthermore, although not a voting member of the session, an associate pastor should be regularly invited to attend its meetings with full right of discussion. An associate pastor (in contrast to a co-pastor) does not alternate in moderating the session with the pastor (see G. XI, 5), but ordinarily would be the first called upon to preside in the absence or illness of the pastor. (See G. XI, 3, and Chapter IV, A, 3, a, this manual.)

e. The same process as that of a pastor when he or the congregation desires to dissolve the relationship. (See G. XXI, 1.)

3. Of an ordained minister employed as an assistant pastor.

a. A written agreement between himself and the session whereby he is engaged to assist the pastor, in one or more parts of his work, which agreement shall be approved by the presbytery, the terms of which may not be changed without the approval of the presbytery. (See G. XX, 1, e.)

b. A service of recognition under the authority of the session. (See C. W., p. 242.)

c. Supervision of his work by the pastor in consultation with the elders.

d. Regular invitations to attend session meetings. Although he has no legal right to attend meetings of the session, he ordinarily ought to be present because of the counsel he may bring to it and for his own benefit when he may be called upon to moderate it (see G. XI, 3, and Chapter IV, A, 3, a, this manual) or later regularly to moderate a session when he is called to a pastorate of his own.

e. An assistant pastor, like a pastor and an associate pastor, not under the ecclesiastical discipline of the session, but a member of the presbytery and subject to its discipline.

f. Adequate notice by the session of its desire to terminate his employment, which termination shall have the approval of the presbytery before becoming effective.

4. Of an ordained minister invited by the session and appointed by the presbytery as a stated supply.

a. A stated supply has the rights of a pastor with the following exceptions:

(1) He may not moderate the session or a congregational meeting unless he is a member of the presbytery and appointed by the presbytery so to do. (See G. XX, 1, g.)

(2) His appointment is for no more than twelve months at a time and must be renewed by the presbytery. (See G. XX, 1, g.)

(3) No formal call is issued by the congregation and no installation is necessary. (See G. XX, 1, g.)

5. Of commissioned church workers. A commissioned church worker is ordinarily a communicant member of the particular church in which he or she is employed and is, therefore, subject to the ecclesiastical discipline of its session. A commissioned church worker is supervised in his or her work by the pastor in consultation with the elders. In order, however, to give dignity and status to these lay positions, the presbytery under the Form of Government confers additional rights to those listed in B, 1, of this chapter, as follows (see G. XXIII):

a. A vote by the congregation authorizing the call of the commissioned church worker. (See G. XXIII, C, 1.)

b. A written call prepared by the session and presented to the presbytery for its approval and presented by the presbytery to the person called. (See G. XXIII, C, 1, 2.)

c. A service of installation by the presbytery. (See G. XXIII, C, 3.)

d. The employment of a commissioned church worker is for an indefinite period (see Form of Call in G. XXIII, C, 1); any change in the terms of the call must be approved by presbytery (see G. XXIII, C, 2); and the dissolution of the relationship must follow G. XXIII, D, 1:

When any commissioned church worker or the session of any church shall desire the dissolution of the relationship between the session and the commissioned church worker, either party shall have access to the presbytery. Reasons for the desire shall be presented and the other party to the relationship shall be asked to appear before the presbytery to show cause, if any they have, why the presbytery should not approve such dissolution. In no case shall the relationship be dissolved without the action of the presbytery.

HOW TO CALL A NEW PASTOR

A. FIRST STEPS

1. When a church has become vacant by the death or removal of its pastor, it is the duty of the congregation to proceed promptly to the calling of a new pastor. The supervision of vacant churches is under the Constitution assigned by the presbytery to its committee on ministerial relations. (See G. XII, 25; XXII, 3; and XXVII, 1–4.) The elders should, therefore, promptly be in touch with that committee through its chairman (a neighboring pastor of the presbytery will supply his name and address) in order that the church may get off to a right start both in its program during the interim between pastorates and in its search for a new pastor. The elders should ascertain from the chairman of presbytery's committee on ministerial relations:

a. The name of the minister appointed by presbytery to moderate the session of the church while it is vacant.

b. A convenient date for an early meeting of the session to call a meeting of the congregation *to elect a nominating committee representative of the whole congregation, whose duty it shall be to nominate a minister to the congregation for election as pastor.* [G. XX, 1, a.] (See Chapter II, B, 3, b, this manual, for required notice of this meeting.)

2. The congregation itself has the power to determine the size and membership of this committee, but there is no

reason why the session may not make recommendations as to both. The committee should be large enough to represent the various groups within the congregation, but should not be so large as to be unwieldy. If a large committee is needed and desired, the congregation or the committee itself should elect from its members an executive committee of probably not more than five to do the active work of hearing and interviewing candidates.

3. The first meeting of the nominating committee should ordinarily consist of little more than electing a chairman and other desired officers, consulting with the presbytery's committee on ministerial relations through its chairman or other representatives, and deciding upon its method of securing a sufficient number of names of possible candidates.

4. The nominating committee should realize that it is required by the Constitution to confer with the presbytery's committee on ministerial relations. (See G. XX, 1, a.) Furthermore, it is well to remember from the beginning that presbytery has a legitimate interest in the selection of a pastor of any church within its bounds.

The committee on ministerial relations shall exercise oversight of churches without pastors in the following ways:

. . . By advising churches regarding the calling of a pastor. The committee on ministerial relations shall meet and consult with every committee appointed by a church to nominate a pastor. It shall advise the nominating committee regarding the suitability of any person whose name is to be put before the congregation, and shall have the privilege of nominating suitable persons to the committee. The presbytery shall permit a call to be placed in the hands of a minister only when the nominating committee of the church has thus consulted the committee of

presbytery before the name is presented to the congregation.

Every call must be placed in the hands of the committee on ministerial relations of the presbytery, and if the committee finds it in order, it shall be presented by it to the presbytery with recommendation for final action. [G. XXVII, 4, c.] (See also G. XXII, 3.)

5. The nominating committee should realize that additional help for their task is available. The employed executive of synod or presbytery (if there is one) is glad to assist in the finding of a pastor, as he works in close association with the ministerial relations committee. Also, General Assembly's Department of Ministerial Relations (4294 N. High Street, Columbus 14, Ohio) is in a position to name persons who would be candidates and to secure biographical data on those whose names have been received from other sources.

6. Permission of the presbytery for the session to supply its own pulpit during the interim must also be secured through the chairman of presbytery's committee on ministerial relations. If it appears to the session that some considerable time may be required before the pulpit can be permanently filled, it may seek a so-called "interim pastor." Usually such men are available from among capable pastors honorably retired who can do much besides preaching regularly to help a church through the sometimes difficult period of a pulpit vacancy.

Sessions should note that *ministers and licentiates connected with the presbyteries of this Church shall be the only persons to be employed as stated supplies in churches without pastors, except in cases of federated churches.* [G. XXII, 2.] Candidates studying at nearby seminaries may also be used as regular supplies of vacant churches with the approval of presbytery and with the sanction and under the guidance of their instructors. (See G. XVIII, 6.)

A part of the task of presbytery's committee on ministerial relations is that it *shall, in consultation with the session, . . . arrange for the supply of the pulpit.* [G. XXII, 3.]

In connection with the rules above, it should be understood that an "interim pastor" is a regular supply. Previously, "ministers of other Churches in correspondence with the General Assembly" might be used as occasional supplies or in staff relationship, if presbytery approved. (See G. XVI, 1, g (P), and G. XXI, 3 (P).) Presently, no such provision is to be found in the Constitution; thus limiting all supplies to ministers and licentiates of this Church, except in unusual situations, of which the presbytery must be the judge. Consultation with the presbytery's committee on ministerial relations is required in all such matters, as indicated above, and will be most helpful.

Previously, before the present closer co-operation between the committee of the local church and the presbytery through the committee on ministerial relations, there were sufficient reasons for the Constitution to provide for the assumption by presbytery of full responsibility for appointing pulpit supplies in a local church after it had been without a pastor for twelve months. (See G. XXI, 4 (P).)

B. NEXT STEPS AND CONCLUSION

1. The nominating committee in consultation with the presbytery's committee on ministerial relations proceeds as rapidly as possible to gather a list of candidates for the pulpit, to correspond with them, to make preliminary selection among them, to interview and hear them.

A nominating committee is well advised to heed carefully the counsel of wise ministers in order to avoid mis-

takes into which inexperienced lay people can so easily fall.
The best methods of approach, the best method of arranging to hear a possible candidate, things to avoid such as
playing one candidate against another or appearing to do
so, can be ascertained from the committee on ministerial
relations. From that committee may be learned also any
standing rules of the particular presbytery which may have
relevance to the process of finding and calling a pastor.

Before requesting the session to call a meeting of the
congregation, the nominating committee, having consulted with presbytery's committee on ministerial relations throughout the process of search for a pastor, should
take note: *The presbytery shall permit a call to be placed
in the hands of a minister only when the nominating
committee of the church has thus consulted the committee of presbytery before the name is presented to the congregation.* [G. XXVII, 4, c, par. 1.]

2. *When the committee is ready to report, it shall notify
the session, which shall call a congregational meeting at
the regular place of worship for the purpose of acting on
the report of the nominating committee. Public notice
of the time, place, and purpose of the meeting shall be
given at least one week prior to the appointed time. The
same procedure shall be followed in the selection of an
associate pastor.* [G. XX, 1, a.]

3. *When a congregation is convened for the election of a
pastor or an associate pastor the moderator of the session
or some other minister of the same presbytery appointed
by him shall preside, and the clerk of the session shall act
as secretary. All communicant members in good and
regular standing, but no others, are entitled to vote.*

*The voters being convened, and prayer for divine guid-
ance having been offered, the moderator shall call for the
report of the nominating committee. He shall then put*

the question: "Are you ready to proceed to the election of
a pastor (or associate pastor)?" If they declare themselves
ready, the moderator shall declare the name submitted by
the nominating committee to be in nomination, and shall
give opportunity for nominations from the floor. Both the
nomination of the committee and any nominations from
the floor must first be submitted to the presbytery's committee on ministerial relations. The vote shall be taken by
ballot. In every case a majority of the voters present and
voting shall be required to elect. [G. XX, 2.]

Take note that even nominations from the floor must
first be submitted to the presbytery's committee on ministerial relations. (See immediately above.)

4. On the election of a pastor (or associate pastor), if it
appears that a large minority of the voters are averse to the
candidate who has received a majority of votes, and cannot be induced to concur in the call, the moderator shall
endeavor to dissuade the majority from prosecuting it
further; but if the electors be nearly or quite unanimous,
or if the majority shall insist upon their right to call a
pastor (or associate pastor), the moderator shall proceed
to draw a call in due form, and to have it subscribed by
them, certifying at the same time in writing the number
of those who do not concur in the call, and any facts of
importance, all of which proceedings shall be laid before
the presbytery, together with the call. [G. XX, 4.]

5. See Appendix D, 1, of this manual, for the form of
call.

6. If any church shall choose to subscribe its call by the
ruling elders and deacons, or by a committee, it shall be
at liberty to do so. But it shall, in such case, be fully
certified to the presbytery that the persons signing have
been appointed for that purpose by a public vote of the

congregation, and that the call has been in all other respects prepared as above directed. [G. XX, 5.]

7. *One or more commissioners shall be appointed by the church to present and prosecute the call before their presbytery. When a call has thus been presented, if found in order, and the presbytery deems it for the good of the church, it shall place the call in the hands of the person to whom it is addressed.* [G. XX, 7.]

8. *When a call shall be presented to any minister, candidate, or licentiate, it shall always be viewed as a sufficient petition from the people for his installation. The acceptance of a call by a minister, or candidate, or licentiate, shall always be considered a request on his part to be installed at the same time. And when a candidate or a licentiate shall be ordained in consequence of a call from any congregation, the presbytery shall, at the same time, if practicable, install him pastor of that church.* [G. XX, 8.]

9. *A church desiring to call a pastor (or associate pastor) from his present charge shall, by its commissioners, in person or by letter, represent to the presbytery the ground on which it pleads his removal. The presbytery, having heard all the parties, may, upon viewing the whole matter, either recommend them to desist from prosecuting the call, or may order it to be delivered to the minister to whom it is addressed, with or without advice, or it may decline to place the call in his hands, as it shall appear most for the peace and edification of the Church at large, or it may refer the whole matter to the synod for advice and direction; and no pastor or associate pastor shall be transferred without his own consent. If the parties are not ready to have action taken upon the matter issued at the meeting then in progress, a written citation shall be*

given the minister and his church to appear before the presbytery at its next meeting. This citation shall be read from the pulpit in that church, immediately before the benediction is pronounced, at least two Sabbaths before said meeting. [G. XX, 9.]

10. If the call be to a minister, or candidate, or licentiate of another presbytery, the commissioners appointed to prosecute the call shall produce in person, or by letter, an attested certificate from their own presbytery that it has been laid before that body and found in order, and that permission has been granted them to prosecute it before the presbytery to which he belongs. If his presbytery thinks it expedient to present the call to him, it may be accordingly presented; and no minister, candidate, or licentiate shall receive a call but through the hands of his own presbytery. [G. XX, 10.]

11. If the church, or other field of labor, to which a minister, candidate, or licentiate is called be under the jurisdiction of a different presbytery, on his acceptance of a call he shall be furnished with the proper testimonials and required to repair promptly to that presbytery, in order that he may be regularly inducted into his office. [G. XX, 11.]

12. From all the above it should be clear that the Presbyterian Church has been very careful to provide in its Constitution a most detailed process in the election and calling and installation of a pastor. The chief purpose of these detailed provisions is to assure all the members of the church and the presbytery that a wise selection will be made by the nominating committee and the congregation. Although undue delay in the replacing of a pastor is often a great harm to a church, thoughtless and undue haste may harm the church much more.

X

WHEN THERE IS TROUBLE

No law or manual of law can prevent trouble and sharp division of opinion arising from time to time in a church. When there is unresolved division within a church, the cause is very often the unwillingness of one party or the other or both to seek the guidance of the Holy Spirit in the matter. The protagonists on the two sides of a church division often make the mistake of trying to use the law to win a victory over the opposition. Such a victory is very costly to the Church of Jesus Christ.

The right resolving of a division of opinion within a church depends under God on a sufficient number of persons who are unwilling to take sides between persons and interests, but who will actively seek under the guidance of God to find the correct way, that is to say, the legal way, to resolve the difficulty in order that the breach may be healed and the congregation go forward in its work and witness for Jesus Christ.

It should not be surprising that church quarrels are sometimes even more bitter than quarrels among other groups of human beings. Church members are human and sinners and become very emotional when their religious beliefs, practices, or actions are involved.

The purpose of this chapter is to give guidance to those within a particular church who really want to find God's answer to the trouble, who are willing to listen fairly and carefully to others with whom they differ, and who, as members of the Christian fellowship, are willing to abide by the decision once it is finally made by Constitutional process. If that decision seems wrong to them, provision is made for complaint or appeal of decisions to the higher courts of the Church, and further provision is made for conscientious protest for those participating as a minority in a decision that goes against their conscience, but that does not appear to offer legal grounds for appeal or complaint. Let no one expect to find in this manual, or anywhere in Presbyterian law, a tool to win an ecclesiastical battle. Before beginning in any legal process suggested in this chapter, let each person read carefully the first chapter of this manual, examine his own heart and the purity of his motives, and pray to God for guidance.

A. WHEN ELDERS DISAGREE

1. If one or more elders find themselves in the minority in regard to an administrative matter that has been decided by the session:

a. They have the right to complain formally to the presbytery if they believe that the action was both unwise and unlawful under the Constitution in any of its parts, which Constitution includes the Confession of Faith, the Larger and Shorter Catechisms, the Form of Government, the Book of Discipline, and the Directory for Worship. Such complaint should not be made lightly, nor is there room in the Church for a litigious spirit. But, if the minority really feels that the session has erred in any matter of vital importance to the life of the Church, this provision for complaint to the presbytery is properly used.

The following steps must be observed in making such a complaint:

(1) Written notice of complaint shall be given to the clerk of the session within ten days after the action of the session to be complained of, or in case of his death, absence, or disability, to the moderator of the session.

(See D. XII, 9.) (See Appendix F, 1 of this manual, for form of notice of complaint.)

If the notice of complaint is signed by at least one third of the members recorded as present when the decision complained of was made, or by one third of the whole membership of the session, the execution of the decision shall be stayed until the final issue of the case in the presbytery, synod, or General Assembly. (See D. XII, 15.)

(2) The complaint itself with the reasons therefor must be lodged with the stated clerk of the presbytery within thirty days after the written notice of the complaint has been given to the clerk of the session. (See D. XII, 10.) (See Appendix F, 2 of this manual for form of complaint.)

The following actions are required of the clerk of the session and the session when its action is complained of:

(1) Within thirty days after the receipt of written notice of the complaint, the clerk of the session shall lodge it, together with the records of his minutes and all other papers pertaining to the case, with the stated clerk of the presbytery. If this is not done, the presbytery has power to censure the session and issue such orders, pending the production by the session of the record and papers and the determination of the complaint, as may be necessary to preserve the rights of the complainants. (See D. XII, 11.)

(2) One or more of its members are appointed by the session to represent it in the presbytery when the case is heard. (See D. XII, 14.) Either the majority or the minority of the session may secure at their own expense copies of the complaint from the stated clerk of the presbytery. (See D. XII, 10.)

The complaint will be decided in the presbytery according to the following procedure:

When the higher judicatory finds that a complaint is in order, and that sufficient reasons for proceeding to its determination have been assigned, the judiciary, or a judicial commission duly elected by it, shall adopt the following procedure:

(1) *The complaint, and the reasons therefor, shall be read.*

(2) *The record of the action against which the complaint is made, and so much of the record of the lower judiciary as may be pertinent, shall be read.*

(3) *The parties shall be heard, the complainants having the right of opening and closing the argument.*

(4) *Opportunity shall be given to the members of the higher judiciary or judicial commission to be heard.*

(5) *The vote shall then be taken without debate separately on each reason assigned in the complaint.* [D. XII, 12.]

The effect of a complaint if sustained may be the reversal, in whole or in part, of the action or decision complained of. When a complaint is sustained, the lower judiciary shall be directed as to further proceedings in the case. [D. XII, 13.]

The parties to a complaint shall be known in the higher judicatories as the complainant and the respondent—the latter being the judiciary complained of, which should always be represented by one or more of its members appointed for that purpose, who may be assisted by counsel. [D. XII, 14.]

Neither the majority nor the minority members of the session shall circulate, or cause to be circulated among the members of the presbytery, any written or printed arguments or briefs upon the matter in question before the presbytery before the disposition of the question by the presbytery, except at the request or direction of the presbytery. (See D. XII, 3.)

b. If one or more elders find themselves in a minority on a matter that has been decided by the session, which does not appear subject to successful complaint, or appeal, they may dissent or protest. (See D. XI.)

A dissent is a declaration by one or more members expressing disagreement with an action or decision. It must be made during the same meeting of the session at which the action or decision dissented from is taken, and the clerk shall enter it in the minutes of the meeting. (See D. XI, 1.)

A protest is a more formal declaration made by one or more members of the session, bearing testimony against what is believed to be an irregular or errroneous proceeding, decision, or judgment, accompanied by the reasons therefor. It shall be entered at the same meeting of the session during which the action protested is taken, and the reasons on which it is founded shall be transmitted to the clerk of the session within ten days. (See D. XI, 2.)

If a protest is couched in decorous and respectful language, and is without offensive reflections or insinuations against the judicatory, it shall be entered on the records. [D. XI, 3.]

The session against whose action a protest is taken may prepare an answer, which shall be entered on the minutes, to any protest that imputes to it principles or reasonings which its action does not impart. Leave may then be given to the person or persons protesting, if they desire it, to modify their protest; and the answer of the session may also, in consequence, be modified. This shall end the matter. (See D. XI, 4.)

The admission of a protest by a judicatory does not justify the person protesting in disobedience and nonsubmission, but implies no more than a recognition of his right to satisfy his conscience. [D. XI, 5.]

2. The procedure under 1, a, above, is confined to any delinquency action, or decision of the session in the exercise of administrative discipline. Any actions of the session that impinge upon the rights of individual members of

the church or of the session must initially be taken by full judicial process. (See Chapter IV of this manual, section B, 3, d.) Whenever a session enters into judicial discipline, the member tried may appeal (not complain of) the action to the presbytery. In view of the infrequency of this process at the session level, this manual does not attempt to treat it, nor the method of appeal. A careful study of the Book of Discipline itself must be made in order to protect the rights of a member who is tried by a session in judicial discipline. See also *Presbyterian Law for the Presbytery*.

B. WHEN MEMBERS OF A PARTICULAR CHURCH DISAGREE WITH ACTIONS TAKEN BY THE SESSION

Church members must recall the powers of the session (see this manual, Chapter IV) and the limitations of the powers of the congregation (see this manual, Chapter II) before they decide to take issue with actions of the church session.

1. When, however, a member or members of a church believe that their session has exceeded, wrongly used, or been delinquent in the use of its powers in the church, they have the right to petition presbytery to visit the church and redress the evil that has allegedly arisen. (See G. XII, 7.)

2. If the elders of a church are generally not representing the will of the congregation, the congregation may refuse to approve any request for exemption from the rotary system (see Chapter III in this manual, A, 2 (2) and (5)) and thus elect some new elders.

C. WHEN SESSION AND TRUSTEES DISAGREE

For the relationship of these two bodies within the church, see Chapters IV and VI of this manual. If all informal means of adjusting differences have failed, it is normally best for the two boards to submit their differences to the congregation for direction in matters of policy within the provisions of the Constitution, or to submit mooted Constitutional questions to the presbytery for counsel and direction.

If the two boards are unwilling to settle differences in the above fashion, it must be remembered that the session has the power to cite and try the trustees as members of the church under its jurisdiction and, if found guilty of offenses under the Constitution, to suspend or excommunicate them, thereby making them ineligible longer to hold office. (See G. XI, 6.) It must equally be remembered that the trustees as a body or as individual members have the right to petition presbytery (see B, 1, above), even to the extent of asking presbytery for the removal of the session.

D. WHEN THE PASTOR IS UNSATISFACTORY

1. To the ruling elders. Any ruling elder in active service may properly approach the committee on ministerial relations of the presbytery to initiate investigation by the presbytery as to whether or not the pastoral relation should be dissolved. (See G. XXVII, 3.)

2. To the congregation. A congregation may by resolution ask the presbytery to dissolve the pastoral relation. Courtesy would suggest that a pastor should be informed beforehand of the intention to propose such a resolution so that he, with the approval of the session, may invite another minister to preside at the meeting. (See Chapter II of this manual, section B, 3, d (3).)

Both the above steps are drastic, and neither should be taken without prior attempts to help the pastor amend his ways to the satisfaction of the congregation or to seek another call if he agrees that his ministrations are no longer satisfactory to the church. The members of the church and the ruling elders should remember before taking any such decision with regard to their pastor that he has rights as well as duties (see Chapter VII of this manual) and that he is subject to the discipline of his presbytery and not to that of the congregation or session. It may be that complaints about the pastor will lead, not to his removal, but to the discipline of those who complain.

A

SUGGESTED BYLAWS OF A CONGREGATION FOR A MEETING

For an ecclesiastical meeting or for a meeting both ecclesiastical and corporation in those states which permit. [Based on this manual, especially Chapter II, B, 3.]

1. The .... (United) Presbyterian Church of .... being a particular congregation of The United Presbyterian Church in the United States of America recognizes that the Constitution of said Church, is in all its provisions, obligatory upon it and its members.

2. There shall be an annual meeting of the congregation in the church edifice on the .... for the transaction of any business properly coming before such meeting.

3. Special meetings may be called by the session or the presbytery. Such calls shall state clearly the purpose of such special meeting, and no other matter save that specified in the call may be considered.

4. Public notice of the time, place, and purpose of all meetings of the congregation shall be given at least one week prior to the appointed time.

5. The pastor shall preside. If the church is vacant, or if the pastor and the elders agree that the subjects to be discussed require it, or if the pastor is ill or is otherwise unable to be present, a minister of .... Presbytery shall be invited by the session to preside. This

invitation shall be cleared through the ministerial relations committee of .... Presbytery.

6. The clerk of the session shall be secretary of the meetings of the congregation. In his inability to attend, the session shall designate a secretary in his stead.

7. All communicant members in good and regular standing shall be entitled to vote at congregational meetings affecting the ecclesiastical affairs of the church and also on all matters affecting the corporate affairs unless otherwise provided by the laws of the state governing its incorporation.

8. Voting by proxy is not allowed.

9. Meetings shall be conducted in accordance with the General Rules for Judicatories adopted by the General Assembly of The United Presbyterian Church in the United States of America, so far as they apply, and when they do not apply, according to usual legislative rules of order.

10. All meetings shall be opened and closed with prayer.

11. A quorum shall consist of the moderator, secretary, and .... eligible voters.

12. There shall be .... elders divided into three equal classes, one class of whom shall be elected each year at the annual meeting for a three-year term. No elder shall serve on the session for consecutive terms, either full or partial, aggregating more than six years; but shall be ineligible to be elected to a new term until .... year(s) shall have elapsed.

13. There shall be .... deacons divided into three classes, one class of whom shall be elected each year at the annual meeting for a three-year term. No deacon shall serve on the board of deacons for consecutive terms, either full or partial, aggregating more than six years; but shall be ineligible to be elected to a new term until .... year(s) shall have elapsed.

14. Vacancies on the session or board of deacons may be filled at a special meeting of the congregation or at the annual meeting, as the session may determine.

15. (For those churches only in which the corporation and ecclesiastical meetings are united.) There shall be .... trustees divided into three equal classes, one class of whom shall be elected each year at the annual meeting for a three-year term. No trustee shall serve on the board of trustees for consecutive terms, either full or partial, aggregating more than six years; but shall be ineligible to be elected to a new term until .... year(s) shall have elapsed.

16. There shall be a representative nominating committee chosen in accordance with the Form of Government. (See Chapter III in this manual.) This committee shall bring to the annual meeting nominations of one eligible person only for each office to be filled. Additional nominations of qualified persons may be made from the floor by any eligible voter. (See G. XVII, 1 (2).)

17. The above rules are based on the Constitution, and may be amended only as follows: Rule 2 is subject to amendment with respect to date, hour, and place of meeting only. Rule 16 is subject to amendment only as to the number of nominations which shall be presented for each office. Rules 1, 3, 4, 5, 6, 7, 8, 9, 10, and 14 are not subject to amendment.

NOTE: The Charter or Articles of Incorporation of a particular Presbyterian church should be as simple as possible (since amendment is usually difficult) and ought to contain the following sentence or its legal equivalent:

"This corporation is organized for the purpose of supporting worship of Almighty God and instruction in the Christian religion, according to the Constitution of The United Presbyterian Church in the United States of America."

B

SUGGESTED BYLAWS OF A CORPORATION

[Based on this manual, especially Chapter II, B.]

1. The bylaws of the .... (United) Presbyterian Church of .... as a corporation shall always be subject to the Constitution and laws of the State of ...., and also to the Constitution of The United Presbyterian Church in the United States of America.

2. There shall be an annual meeting of the corporation at .... o'clock (or immediately following adjournment of the ecclesiastical meeting of the congregation) on the .... day of ...., for the transaction of any business properly coming before such meeting.

3. Special meetings may be called by the trustees and shall be called by the trustees at the request of the session. Presbytery may call a special meeting or authoritatively direct the trustees so to do. All such calls shall state clearly the purpose of such meeting, and no other matter save that specified in the call may be considered.

4. Public notice of the time, place, and purpose of all meetings of the corporation as prepared by the trustees (or presbytery) shall be publicly announced from the pulpit on the two successive Sundays next preceding the day of such meeting.

5. The president of the board of trustees or other member of the board designated by it shall convene meetings

of the corporation and shall preside unless by majority vote the corporation shall elect another of its membership in his place.

6. The secretary of the board of trustees shall be the secretary of meetings of the corporation. In his inability to serve, the board of trustees shall designate a substitute.

7. All communicant members of the church in good and regular standing shall be entitled at all meetings of the church to vote on all matters affecting the ecclesiastical affairs of the church, and also on all matters affecting the corporate affairs (unless otherwise provided by the laws of the state governing its incorporation).

8. Voting by proxy is not allowed. (Omit in states where such voting is expressly directed by statute.)

9. A quorum shall consist of .... eligible voters.

10. There shall be .... trustees (this may be subject to limitations of the charter or articles of incorporation), divided into three equal classes, one class of whom shall be elected each year at the annual meeting for a three-year term. No trustee shall serve on the board of trustees for consecutive terms, either full or partial, aggregating more than six years; but shall be ineligible to be elected to a new term until .... year(s) shall have elapsed.

11. No one shall be elected trustee who is not a communicant member of full age in good standing of this church.

12. Vacancies on the board of trustees by reason of death or resignation shall be filled at the next annual meeting of the corporation unless the trustees decide by resolution to call a special meeting for the purpose.

13. Trustees shall be nominated, one only for each vacancy, by the nominating committee of the church charged with this responsibility by the Constitution, which provides that a representative of the board of trustees shall

be on such nominating committee. Additional nominations may be made by any eligible voter.

14. The duties of trustees shall be those only delegated to them by the laws of the State of ...., the Constitution of The United Presbyterian Church in the United States of America, the session of this church, and by formal actions of a meeting of this corporation.

15. The trustees shall report annually to the corporation:

a. The receipts and payments for the previous fiscal year.

b. An estimate of expenses and income for the year ahead.

c. New business necessary to be undertaken for the welfare of the congregation.

d. An exhibit of the real property, trust funds, and other resources of the congregation.

16. The books and accounts of the trustees shall not be open to the inspection of members of the corporation, but the session shall at all times have access thereto.

17. These bylaws may be amended subject to the charter of the corporation, the laws of the State of ......
.........., and the Constitution of The United Presbyterian Church in the United States of America at any annual meeting, or at any special meeting, by a two-thirds vote of the voters present, provided that a full reading of the proposed changes (or a printed distribution of the same) shall have been made in connection with the call of the meeting. Rules 1, 3, 4, 5, 7, 8, 10, 11, and 16 are not subject to amendment because of the provisions of the Constitution of The United Presbyterian Church in the United States of America. Rule 2 may be amended only as to time and place.

DOCKET FOR MEETINGS OF SESSION

The docket of business for session meetings should be prepared by the clerk, and handed by him to the moderator at the opening of each session. The following form is suggested, and contains the more important items of business likely to come before a session, except those connected with judicial cases. It can be modified to suit specific needs:

1. Opening prayer.
2. Calling of roll.
3. Reading and approval of minutes.
4. Communications from presbytery, synod, and General Assembly.
5. Reports of permanent committees.
6. Reports of special committees.
7. Report of pastor.
8. Report of clerk.
9. Report of treasurer.
10. Examination and reception of members.
11. Dismissal of members.
12. Arrangements for Lord's Supper when necessary.
13. Report to presbytery when in order.
14. Report of commissioner to presbytery or synod.
15. Unfinished business.
16. Miscellaneous business.
17. Adjournment.
18. Prayer and benediction.

D

FORMS FOR USE BY THE CONGREGATION

1. The call of a pastor. *The call shall be in the following or like form, namely:* *

The .... (United) Presbyterian Church of ...., being, on sufficient grounds, well satisfied of the ministerial qualifications of you, ..., and having good hopes from our knowledge of you, that your ministrations in the gospel will be profitable to our spiritual interests, do earnestly call and desire you to undertake the office of pastor in said congregation, promising you in the discharge of your duty all proper support, encouragement, and obedience in the Lord. And that you may be free from worldly care and avocations, we, on our part, promise and oblige ourselves to pay you the sum of .... yearly in regular payments during the time of your being and continuing the regular pastor of this church, together with free use of the manse and .... vacation each year. And we agree to pay or to continue to pay monthly or quarterly in advance to the Board of Pensions a sum equivalent to that requisite per cent of said salary which may be fixed by the General Assembly of The United Presbyterian Church in the United States of America for participation in the (Service Pension Plan). And we promise and oblige ourselves to

[* A printed form may be purchased from the Division of Publication of the Board of Christian Education, Witherspoon Building, Philadelphia 7, Pennsylvania.]

review with you the adequacy of this compensation annually, prior to the adoption of the church budget.

In testimony whereof we have respectively subscribed our names this .... day of ....
......, A.D. ....

(Signatures)

I, A.B., having moderated the congregational meeting which extended a call to .... for his ministerial services, do certify that the call has been made in all respects according to the rules laid down in the Form of Government, and that the persons who signed the foregoing call were authorized to do so by vote of the congregation.

....

Moderator of the meeting.

[G. XX, 6.]

2. The call of an associate pastor. *The call shall be in the following or like form, namely:*

The .... (United) Presbyterian Church of .....
....., being, on sufficient grounds, well satisfied of the ministerial qualifications of you, ..., and having good hopes from our knowledge of you, that your ministrations in the gospel will be profitable to our spiritual interests, do earnestly call and desire you to undertake the office of associate pastor in said congregation, promising you in the discharge of your duty all proper support, encouragement, and obedience in the Lord. And that you may be free from worldly care and avocations, we, on our part, promise and oblige ourselves to pay you the sum of .... yearly in regular payments during the time of your being and continuing the associate pastor of this church, together with free use of a manse and .... vacation each year. And we agree to pay or to continue to pay monthly or quarterly in advance to the Board of Pensions a sum equivalent to that requi-

site per cent of said salary which may be fixed by the General Assembly of The United Presbyterian Church in the United States of America for participation in the (Service Pension Plan). And we promise and oblige ourselves to review with you the adequacy of this compensation annually, prior to the adoption of the church budget.

In testimony whereof we have respectively subscribed our names this .... day of ....
......, A.D. ....

(Signatures)

I, A.B., *having moderated the congregational meeting which extended a call to .... for his ministerial services, do certify that the call has been made in all respects according to the rules laid down in the Form of Government, and that the persons who signed the foregoing call were authorized to do so by vote of the congregation.*

....
Moderator of the meeting.
[G. XX, 6.]

FORMS FOR USE BY SESSION

The following printed forms for use by session are available from the Division of Publication, Board of Christian Education, Witherspoon Building, Philadelphia 7, Pennsylvania:

Certificates of Dismission and Reception

Certificates of Church Membership

Certificates of Ordination of Ruling Elders or Deacons

Baptismal Certificates

Westminster Church Register, Loose-leaf or Bound Edition

Loose-leaf Record for Typewritten Minutes of Session

Minutes of Session in Bound Form

F

OTHER FORMS

1. Form of Notice of Complaint

In the matter of the action of the session of ......
.... Church respecting .... (here
state action), the undersigned hereby give(s) notice of
his (their) intention to complain to ....
Presbytery as to aforesaid action.

.... (Signature(s)).

Date:................

To the Clerk of Session of

.... (United) Presbyterian Church.

2. Form of Complaint

In the matter of the action of the session of ......
.... Church of .... respecting
.... (here state action), the undersigned
hereby complain(s) to .... Presbytery in
the above entitled matter, and for the reasons in support
of such complaint state(s) the following: (Here state reasons for complaint in plain, simple language and consecutive order).

....
(Signature(s) of Complainant(s)).

Date:................

To the Stated Clerk of

.... Presbytery.

G

GENERAL RULES FOR JUDICATORIES

(Adopted by the General Assembly of 1821, with Amendments to 1934, and revised in 1958 at the time of the merger of the Presbyterian Church in the United States of America with the United Presbyterian Church of North America.)

[The following "General Rules for Judicatories," not having been submitted to the presbyteries, make no part of the Constitution of the Presbyterian Church. Yet the General Assembly of 1821, considering uniformity in proceedings in all the subordinate judicatories as greatly conducive to order and dispatch in business, having revised and approved these Rules, recommended them to all the lower judicatories of the Church for adoption. Succeeding Assemblies have also approved these Rules, making amendments from time to time.]

[It will be understood that the words in black-faced type, which immediately precede each Rule and summarize its contents, form no part of the Rule itself.]

OF OPENING THE SESSIONS

Meeting to be opened with prayer:

1. The moderator shall take the chair precisely at the hour to which the judicatory stands adjourned; shall immediately call the members to order; and on the appearance of a quorum, the session shall be opened with prayer.

(Note: the term "session" is used for a sitting of a judicatory for a portion of a day.)

Those eligible to preside if moderator be absent:

2. If a quorum be assembled at the time appointed, and the moderator be absent, the last moderator present, be-

ing a commissioner, or if there be none, the senior member present, shall be requested to take his place without delay, until a new election.

Procedure when no quorum present:

3. If a quorum be not assembled at the hour appointed, any two members shall be competent to adjourn from time to time, that an opportunity may be given for a quorum to assemble.

OF THE MODERATOR

Moderator a member of the judicatory:

4. The moderator shall be a member of the judicatory over which he is chosen to preside.

Authority possessed by moderator:

5. The moderator shall be considered as possessing, by delegation from the whole body, all authority necessary for the preservation of order, for convening and adjourning the judicatory, and for directing its operations according to the rules of the Church.

Moderator to preserve order and dispatch business:

6. It shall be the duty of the moderator, at all times, to preserve order, and to endeavor to conduct all business before the judicatory to a speedy and proper result.

Moderator to keep schedule of business assigned for particular times:

7. It shall be the duty of the moderator carefully to keep note of the several articles of business which may be assigned for particular days, and to call them up at the time appointed.

Moderator may appoint a vice-moderator:

8. The moderator may appoint a vice-moderator, who may occupy the chair at his request, and otherwise assist him in the discharge of his duties.

Moderator appointing committees:

9. The moderator shall appoint all committees, except in those cases in which the judicatory shall decide otherwise.

Moderator may call any member to chair:

10. The moderator may call any member to the chair, to preside temporarily.

Moderator shall propose every subject:

11. The moderator shall propose to the judicatory every subject of deliberation that comes before it.

Moderator to put the question and announce the decision:

12. In all questions the moderator shall give a concise and clear statement of the object of the vote; when deliberations on a question are ended he shall put the question and call for the vote; and the vote being taken shall then declare how the question is decided.

Moderator recognizing speakers:

13. The moderator shall always announce the names of members rising to speak, prevent them from interrupting each other, and require them, in speaking, always to address the chair.

Moderator discussing and deciding points of order:

14. The moderator may speak to points of order in preference to other members, rising from his seat for that purpose, and shall decide questions of order subject to an appeal to the judicatory, without debate, by any two members.

When moderator may or may not vote:

15. When a vote is taken by ballot in any judicatory, the moderator shall vote with the other members. But he

shall not vote in any other case, unless the judicatory be equally divided, when he shall possess the deciding vote; if he be not willing to decide he shall put the question a second time; and if the judicatory be again equally divided, and he decline to give his vote, the question shall be lost.

Right of appeal from moderator's decision:

16. If any member consider himself aggrieved by a decision of the moderator, it shall be his privilege to appeal to the judicatory, and the question on the appeal shall be taken without debate.

Moderator to serve until successor inducted into office:

17. The moderator shall serve until his successor be inducted into office, and may perform such administrative duties as are assigned to him by the judicatory.

OF THE STATED CLERK

Stated clerk to form complete roll for moderator:

18. It shall be the duty of the stated clerk, as soon as possible after the commencement of the sessions of every judicatory, to form a complete roll of the members present, and put the same into the hands of the moderator. Whenever any additional members take their seats, he shall add their names in their proper places to the said roll.

Duties of stated clerk and committee on bills and overtures:

19. It shall be the duty of the stated clerk immediately to file all papers, in the order in which they have been read, with proper endorsements, and to keep them in perfect order. The stated clerk shall receive all overtures, memorials, and miscellaneous papers addressed to the judicatory; shall make record of the same and deliver them to the committee on bills and overtures for appropriate disposition or reference.

OF THE ORDER OF BUSINESS

Minutes of last meeting:

20. The minutes of the last meeting of the judicatory shall be presented at the commencement of its sessions, and, if requisite, read and corrected.

Committee on bills and overtures:

21. The committee on bills and overtures shall have the floor on the reassembling of the judicatory after each recess and adjournment, to report its recommendations as to orders of business or reference of papers, and this right of the committee shall take precedence of the orders of the day. This committee shall report the papers retained by it as well as those recommended for reference to other committees, and no committee shall report on matters which have not been referred to it by the judicatory.

Unfinished business:

22. Business left unfinished at the last sitting is ordinarily to be taken up first.

OF COMMITTEES

Appointment:

23. When a committee is appointed to deliberate upon a subject, it is the rule to appoint thereon members holding different views.

When a committee is appointed to carry out a decision of the house, it is customary to appoint thereon only those who can support the action taken.

Committee chairmanship:

24. The first person named on any committee shall be considered as the chairman thereof, whose duty it shall be to convene the committee and preside therein; and in case of his absence, or inability to act, the second named member shall take his place and perform his duties.

Chairman may debate and vote:

25. The chairman of a committee may debate and vote, and may also act as clerk.

Quorum of a committee:

26. The quorum of a committee is, in legislative practice, a majority of the members.

Filling vacancies in a committee:

27. Committees cannot fill vacancies in their membership. Only the house or the moderator can act.

Committee must receive permission to withdraw:

28. Committees must receive permission from the house to withdraw.

Discharging a committee:

29. Committees of the judicatories are ordinarily discharged by the reception of their report. The Standing Committees of the General Assembly, however, are discharged at the final session by vote of the house. Special committees of the General Assembly are discharged with the adjournment of the Assembly unless continued by specific action.

Committee reports:

30. The report of a committee, when received or accepted by the General Assembly, is the property of the General Assembly, and should be handed to the Stated Clerk, with all accompanying papers.

The words "received or accepted" used for the reception of reports, do not imply adoption.

The minority of a committee may submit their views in writing, either together or each member separately, but a minority report can be considered and acted upon only by moving it as a substitute for the report of the committee.

OF MOTIONS

Motions seconded, repeated, read aloud, written:

31. A motion must be seconded, and afterward repeated by the moderator, or read aloud, before it is debated; and every motion shall be reduced to writing, if the moderator or any member require it.

Mover of motion entitled to floor:

32. The mover of a motion is entitled to the floor if he so desire, after the moderator has stated the question.

Withdrawal of a motion:

33. Any member who shall have made a motion shall have liberty to withdraw it, with the consent of his second, before any debate has taken place thereon; but not afterward, without the leave of the judicatory.

Dividing a motion:

34. If a motion under debate contain several parts, any two members may have it divided, and a question taken on each part.

Privileged motions:

35. In ordinary legislative business the privileged motions are (1) to fix the time for next sitting, (2) to adjourn, (3) questions of privilege, (4) to take up special orders.

Motions admissible when a question is under debate:

36. When a question is under debate, no motion shall be received, unless to adjourn, to docket, to lay on the table, to postpone indefinitely, to postpone to a definite day, to commit, or to amend; which several motions shall have precedence in the order in which they are herein arranged; and the motion for adjournment shall always be in order.

Motions to lay on the table:

37. A distinction shall be observed between a motion to lay on the table for the present and a motion to lay on the table unconditionally, viz.: A motion to lay on the table for the present shall be taken without debate; and, if carried in the affirmative, the effect shall be to place the subject on the docket, and it may be taken up and considered at any subsequent time. But a motion to lay on the table unconditionally shall be taken without debate; and, if carried in the affirmative, it shall not be in order to take up the subject during the same meeting of the judicatory, without a vote of reconsideration.

Calling the question:

38.(a) When any member shall call for "the question," the moderator shall, without debate, put the vote, "Is the court ready for the question?" If the call be seconded by a majority of the members present, the vote shall immediately be taken on the pending question, whatever it may be, without further debate.

(b) The previous question shall be put in this form, namely, "Shall the main question be now put?" It shall only be admitted when demanded by a majority of the members present; and the effect shall be to put an end to all debate and bring the body to a direct vote: first, on a motion to commit the subject under consideration (if such motion shall have been made); secondly, if the motion for commitments does not prevail, on pending amendments; and lastly, on the main question.

Motion to reconsider:

39. A question shall not be again called up or reconsidered at the same sessions of the judicatory at which it has been decided, unless by the consent of two thirds of the members who were present at the decision; and unless the motion to reconsider be made and seconded by persons who voted with the majority.

A question shall not again be called up or reconsidered at a meeting of a judicatory subsequent to that at which it was decided unless at least ten days' notice in the case of a session or a presbytery, and at least thirty days' notice in the case of a synod, shall have been given the members of the judicatory through the stated clerk, or in the case of his death or disability through the moderator of the judicatory, of the precise wording of the resolution of reconsideration and of proposed subsequent action, if reconsideration be voted (such as amend, annul, expunge, exscind, rescind). Reconsideration and any proposed subsequent action (such as amend, annul, expunge, exscind, rescind), under the above procedure, may, when the judicatory convenes, be moved or seconded by any member of the judicatory present and a majority vote of the members present shall determine. A matter may be reconsidered the second time, provided that the motion is made and seconded by persons who voted with the majority, and is carried by a two-thirds majority of those previously present and voting on the measure when it was previously before the General Assembly.

(For reconsideration of a matter laid on the table "unconditionally," see Rule 37.)

Indefinite postponement:

40. A subject which has been indefinitely postponed, either by the operation of the previous question or by a motion for indefinite postponement, shall not be again called up during the same sessions of the judicatory, unless by the consent of three fourths of the members who were present at the decision.

OF AMENDMENTS

Amendments and substitutes:

41. An amendment, and also an amendment to an amendment, may be moved on any motion; but a motion to amend an amendment to an amendment shall not be

in order. Action on amendments shall precede action on the original motion. A substitute shall be treated as an amendment.

Amendment laid on the table:

42. An amendment may be laid on the table without affecting another amendment or the original motion.

OF NOMINATIONS

Nominations:

43. A motion may be made to close nominations for any office, whenever time sufficient has been given for the presentation of names. It is competent for the General Assembly, after a vote has been taken for an office without result, to reopen nominations, placing additional candidates before the house.

OF SPEAKERS

Speakers to address moderator and to observe decorum and respect:

44. Every member, when speaking, shall address himself to the moderator, and shall treat his fellow members, and especially the moderator, with decorum and respect.

More than one rising to speak at the same time:

45. If more than one member rise to speak at the same time, the member who is most distant from the moderator's chair shall speak first.

More than three members standing at the same time:

46. When more than three members of the judicatory shall be standing at the same time, the moderator shall require all to take their seats, the person only excepted who may be speaking.

Opposite sides alternating in debate:

47. In the discussion of all matters where the sentiment of the house is divided, it is proper that the floor should

be occupied alternately by those representing the different sides of the question.

Speakers not to be interrupted:

48. No speaker shall be interrupted, unless he be out of order, or for the purpose of correcting mistakes or misrepresentations.

Member called to order:

49. A member called to order does not yield his right to the floor, but should take his seat until the question of order is decided, when he can resume the floor. A second question of order cannot be raised until the first is decided.

Speaker who yields the floor:

50. A member who yields the floor for any purpose is entitled thereto upon the resumption of the business in connection with which he was speaking.

OF LIMITATIONS OF DEBATE

Motions put without debate:

51. Motions to lay on the table, to docket, to take up business, to reconsider, to adjourn, to fix the time of the next session, and the call for the previous question, shall be put without debate; but it shall not be in order for anyone debating another motion to propose the motion to lay on the table or the previous question, at the close of his remarks, unless he shall obtain the floor again for that purpose.

Motions on which members may speak but once or twice:

52. On questions of orders, postponement, or commitment, no member shall speak more than once. On all other questions, each member may speak twice, but not oftener without express leave of the judicatory.

Who has the right to speak last in debate:

53. The member presenting a motion or submitting a report has a right to close the debate.

OF VOTING

Effect of commencing to take a vote:

54. When the moderator has commenced taking the vote, no further debate or remark shall be admitted, unless there has evidently been a mistake, in which case the mistake shall be rectified, and the moderator shall recommence taking the vote.

Effect of deciding to vote at a definite time:

55. If the house shall pass the motion to "vote on a given subject at a time named," speeches shall thereafter be limited to ten minutes. Should the hour for adjournment or recess arrive during the voting it shall be postponed to finish the vote, unless the majority shall vote to adjourn; in which case the voting shall, on the reassembling of the house, take precedence of all other business till it is finished. Under this rule the "yeas and nays" shall not be called except on the final motion to adopt as a whole. This motion to fix a time for voting shall be put without debate.

Calling for the yeas and nays, or for a division:

56. The yeas and nays on any question shall not be recorded, unless required by one third of the members present. If division is called for on any vote, it shall be by a rising vote without a count. If on such a rising vote the moderator is unable to decide, or a quorum rise to second a call for "tellers," then the vote shall be taken by rising, and the count made by tellers, who shall pass through the aisles and report to the moderator the number voting on each side.

Motion for filling blanks:

57. When various motions are made with regard to the filling of blanks with particular numbers or times, the

question shall always be first taken on the highest number and the longest time.

Members declining to vote:

58. Members ought not, without weighty reasons, to decline voting, as this practice might leave the decision of very interesting questions to a small proportion of the judicatory. Silent members, unless excused from voting, must be considered as asquiescing with the majority.

Members excused from voting:

59. A member cannot be excused from voting after the negative of a question is put. The proper time to make the request is immediately at the close of debate, or when the name of a member is called on a yea and nay vote.

Members not to vote on personal interests:

60. Members may not vote on questions affecting their personal interests.

Majority vote required to elect:

61. In all elections it requires a majority of the votes cast to elect.

Vote on appeal from the chair:

62. This appeal is ordinarily put in the following manner: "Shall the decision of the chair stand as the decision of the General Assembly?" A tie vote sustains the chair.

When vote should be retaken:

63. Vote should be retaken if there is evident error and when the tellers disagree.

OF QUESTIONS OF PRIVILEGE

Priority of questions of privilege:

64. Questions of privilege are questions on subjects which affect the rights of the General Assembly or of in-

dividual members, and demand immediate attention. They have priority over all questions except those to fix the time for the next sitting and to adjourn. The chair may decide what questions of this kind to entertain and their priority subject to appeal.

Personal explanation not a question of privilege:

65. A personal explanation is not a "question of privilege" unless it affects the rights of a member.

OF DECORUM

Jurisdiction over members:

66. Every legislative body has the right to call to account its members for objectionable conduct.

Gravity and dignity commended; prolix and desultory speeches to be avoided:

67. It is indispensable that members of ecclesiastical judicatories maintain great gravity and dignity while judicially convened; that they attend closely in their speeches to the subject under consideration, and avoid prolix and desultory harangues; and when they deviate from the subject, it is the privilege of any member, and the duty of the moderator, to call them to order.

Personal reflections not permissible:

68. No member, in the course of debate, shall be allowed to indulge in personal reflections. Also the moderator shall prevent a speaker from deviating from the subject.

Members to refrain from private conversation:

69. Without express permission, no member of a judicatory, while business is going on, shall engage in private conversation; nor shall members address one another, nor any person present, but through the moderator.

Disorderly members subject to reproof:

70. If any member act, in any respect, in a disorderly manner, it shall be the privilege of any member, and the duty of the moderator, to call him to order.

Leave of absence:

71. No member shall retire from any judicatory without the leave of the moderator, nor withdraw from it to return home without the consent of the judicatory.

OF PRIVATE SESSIONS

Private sessions:

72. All judicatories have a right to sit in private on business which, in their judgment, ought not to be matter of public speculation.

OF THE COMMITTEE OF THE WHOLE

Committee of the whole and interlocutory meetings:

73. Every judicatory has a right to resolve itself into a committee of the whole, or to hold what are commonly called interlocutory meetings, in which members may freely converse together without the formalities necessary in their ordinary proceedings. In all such cases the moderator shall name the member who is to preside as chairman. If the committee be unable to agree, a motion may be made that the committee rise, and upon the adoption of such motion the moderator shall resume the chair, and the chairman of the committee shall report what was done, and ask that the committee be discharged, which being allowed, the matter shall be dropped. If the committee shall agree upon the report to be made, or have made progress in the same without coming to a conclusion, the committee may rise, report what has been done, and if the case may require, ask leave to sit again; or the committee of the whole may be dissolved, and the ques-

tion considered by the judicatory in the usual order of business.

Sitting in judicial capacity:

74. Whenever a judicatory is about to sit in a judicial capacity, it shall be the duty of the moderator solemnly to announce, from the chair, that the body is about to pass to the consideration of the business assigned for trial, and to enjoin on the members to recollect and regard their high character as judges of a court of Jesus Christ, and the solemn duty in which they are about to act.

Committee on judicial business:

75. It is expedient that synods and presbyteries appoint a standing committee, to be known as "the committee on judicial business," to whom shall be referred all papers and questions of a judicial nature, and whose duty it shall be to recommend to the judicatory answers to judicial questions and orders of procedure in all judicial cases. The members of the committee on judicial business are not debarred by their appointment from sitting and voting as members of the judicatory.

Procedure in taking cases from inferior judicatories to the General Assembly:

76. Whenever a case is to be taken from an inferior judicatory to the General Assembly, the stated clerk of such inferior judicatory shall, at least twenty days before the meeting of the General Assembly, send a notice concerning such case to the Stated Clerk of the General Assembly, who shall forthwith notify the chairman of the Permanent Judicial Commission, unless the General Assembly shall have ordered otherwise, that the services of the Commission will be needed at the approaching General Assembly; but if no such notice shall be received by the Stated Clerk of the General Assembly, he shall

forthwith notify the chairman of the Permanent Judicial Commission that the services of the Commission will not be needed at the approaching General Assembly.

OF CORRESPONDING MEMBERS

Permanent officers have the rights of corresponding members:

77. The permanent officers of a judicatory shall have the rights of corresponding members in matters touching their several offices.

OF MINUTES

Minutes to be approved:

78. Minutes are to be approved by a motion duly adopted.

Votes required for expunging or correcting minutes:

79. Minutes may be expunged by a unanimous vote. Minutes may be corrected by a majority vote.

OF ADJOURNMENT AND RECESS

Adjournment:

80. The motion to adjourn is not in order when a member has the floor.

The motion to adjourn, when made at the last sitting upon each day, should always include the time on the day following to which the body adjourns.

The business interrupted by adjournment or recess is the first in order after the body reassembles, unless there be a special order on the docket.

The motion to adjourn and to fix the time of the next session are not debatable.

Recess:

81. At the close of a session, provided another session is to follow on the same day, it is customary to move that recess be taken.

OF CLOSING THE SESSIONS

Manner of closing final session:

82. The moderator of every judicatory above the church session, in finally closing its sessions, in addition to prayer, may cause to be sung an appropriate psalm or hymn, and shall pronounce the apostolic benediction.

OF CASES UNPROVIDED FOR

Cases governed by parliamentary law:

83. All cases that may arise, not provided for in the foregoing rules, shall be governed by the general principles of parliamentary law.

OF SUSPENDING THE RULES

Suspending the rules:

84. These rules may be suspended by a two-thirds vote of the judicatory, upon motion duly made.

H

RULES FOR SESSION MINUTES

1. Record the date, time, and place of each meeting; the names of the moderator and the elders present and the names of the absentees.

2. Record the opening and closing of each meeting with prayer.

3. Record the reading and approval of the minutes of the last meeting.

4. Record only that which is vital to the transactions of the meeting.

5. The details of discussions, plans which have not been adopted, suggestions which have not been followed, motions that have been lost, should never be recorded except by special order of the session of which order the records should take note.

6. When a previous action of the session is referred to, the page or pages on which it is recorded should be designated.

7. Avoid erasures, interlineations, and footnotes.

8. Do not insert in the records written or printed matter on separate sheets of paper.

9. Record the administration of the sacrament of the Lord's Supper at the next regular meeting succeeding. In case the sacrament has been administered privately, the name of the elder or elders assisting should be noted.

10. Record the baptism of adults and of infants at the next regular meeting succeeding.

11. Record the full name of applicants for church membership; in case of married females, the maiden name, and wife or widow of; in the case of minors, son or daughter of; and in every case whether baptized; and the name of the church dismissed from, in the case of persons received by letter.

12. Record the full title of the church to which a certificate of dismission is granted, and the full name of the person dismissed with the date of dismissal.

13. Record the name of the elder appointed as a commissioner to synod or presbytery; also the exact period for which he was appointed commissioner; also upon the expiration of his term of service as delegate his report of his attendance and fidelity.

14. The record of each meeting is to be duly attested by the clerk or moderator.

15. When the session of a church finds it necessary to exercise discipline, the Form of Government, the Book of Discipline, and the Digest should be carefully studied by a committee of the session, and if discipline be administered, the minutes of the session must contain such a record of the proceedings had, as will enable the presbytery to know who were disciplined, and why, and how. [See D. V, 14.]

16. Once each year (the official Church year ends Dec. 31) and at the conclusion of the minutes of the meetings of said year, there should be inserted in full the annual tabular statement which the session of the church has made to the presbytery. Also the report made by the session to presbytery of changes in the ruling eldership by death or otherwise; also in outline, the important actions taken at the congregational meetings held during the year.

17. *Every session shall keep registers or rolls of persons admitted to or suspended from the Lord's Table; and of the deaths and other removals of church members, but the names of members shall be placed upon or removed*

from the rolls of the church only by order of the session, and in accordance with the provisions of the Book of Discipline. The session shall also keep a complete register of marriages, and of adult and infant baptisms, with the times of the births of the infants baptized. [G. XI, 13.]

INDEX